FREE to FLY
IT IS YOUR REALITY

Rev Dempsey Harshaw

Copyright © 2011 Rev Dempsey Harshaw

All rights reserved. No part of this book may be used or reproduced by any means, graphic, electronic, or mechanical, including photocopying, recording, taping or by any information storage retrieval system without the written permission of the publisher except in the case of brief quotations embodied in critical articles and reviews.

Balboa Press books may be ordered through booksellers or by contacting:

Balboa Press
A Division of Hay House
1663 Liberty Drive
Bloomington, IN 47403
www.balboapress.com
1-(877) 407-4847

Because of the dynamic nature of the Internet, any web addresses or links contained in this book may have changed since publication and may no longer be valid. The views expressed in this work are solely those of the author and do not necessarily reflect the views of the publisher, and the publisher hereby disclaims any responsibility for them.

The author of this book does not dispense medical advice or prescribe the use of any technique as a form of treatment for physical, emotional, or medical problems without the advice of a physician, either directly or indirectly. The intent of the author is only to offer information of a general nature to help you in your quest for emotional and spiritual well-being. In the event you use any of the information in this book for yourself, which is your constitutional right, the author and the publisher assume no responsibility for your actions.

Any people depicted in stock imagery provided by Thinkstock are models, and such images are being used for illustrative purposes only.
Certain stock imagery © Thinkstock.

ISBN: 978-1-4525-3247-9 (sc)
ISBN: 978-1-4525-3248-6 (e)
ISBN: 978-1-4525-3249-3 (hc)

Library of Congress Control Number: 2011901406

Printed in the United States of America

Balboa Press rev. date: 2/23/2011

DEDICATION

There are a few people that I could mention here but the one that is absolutely obvious and real for me is J Frank Reeve Harshaw. My father was always there to listen to me. He had a unique way of thinking and being a free thinker when it came to life, truth and the scriptures. We spent hours at a time talking about what Bible scriptures were saying and what was between the lines and not being said. We shared things ranging from Spiritual, mystical, paranormal, extraterrestrial, and physics. There was absolutely never a time that I did not know that he loved me unconditionally. My Father always reminded me how important it was in life to put myself in the other person's shoes. Although he is not with me anymore the love and appreciation has not diminished.

Even when we did not agree, he always kept an open mind and more importantly an open heart. He never just dismissed something I said because he thought he was right. At the end of his life in this world, there were some topics of truth that we had spoken about in past conversations. Although he didn't seem to really go along with what I said, he was a person that really did listen and take what was shared to heart. I am sharing this because in one of the last conversations we had about these familiar topics of truth, he replied back to me, "I see what you mean son." It was a very special moment for both of us as we discussed these truths in depth. He never shut himself off to me at anytime for any reason.

I Love you Dad.

CONTENTS

Acknowledgements ix
Preface xi
My Unnamed Angel 1
A Journey of Consciousness 5
Ownership 11
Believing 27
Claiming Your Power 33
    The Prodigal Son
The Myth of Ego 43
Reality and Truth 49
Letters of Infinite Consciousness 59
Nothing Is Real 67
Additional Letters of Consciousness 79
Walking on Water 85
Choice 89
Your Feelings, Your Experience 95
You Are not a Singularity 99
Final Statement 107
Books of Reference 113

ACKNOWLEDGEMENTS

A very important acknowledgement and appreciation that I really am so pleased to give is for Robert Scheinfeld and his book, BUSTING LOOSE from The MONEY GAME.

I am grateful for all of Balboa Press staff and editing department for supporting me in an understanding of what I was really presenting in this book.

Karen Elizabeth as a friend has always been there for me in great support and also came through with the beautiful cover design of this book. I have loving appreciation for my friend Graciela Hernández that has supported me on my journey and for the art work in some of the chapters of this book. My friend Fran Gertler helped to set this book in motion with her recommendations of a publisher as well as assisted editing.

Finally my appreciation goes to Deborah Moreno for always supporting me in my writings as well as so many other friends that have been jewels of support in my world.

Thank you all.

PREFACE

All the following that you are about to read is presented in the understanding that there is only one God, one Spirit, and one life. There are not good and evil life forces out there. There is only one Consciousness. If your beliefs are in any separateness or that duality is the reality, this could bring up and create some challenges on a very deep level. But, I know that wonderfully nothing is set in stone, and I encourage you to follow your heart, feelings, and intuition.

Before I go further, I want to make it clear that some of what you will read here is possibly easier for some to be understood and accepted in the understanding of quantum physics. But, it is not necessarily so. The Toltec that were of the Aztec culture and times were a very spiritual, artistic, and creative people, who believed the waking state of life was the dream while the sleeping state was the reality. They did not base this on any science. Quantum physics demonstrates that the basic physics—wherein we have been taught the appearance of form and its laws—is not really true in the reality of what the universe is. It is not my intention to elaborate on physics of the quantum aspects of what appears to be the reality of things, but to note that in this quantum science, nothing is real with actual real existence. All is considered more like a thought. I will refer you to some books in the reference section. I am speaking here on a more spiritual, intuitive basis, and at times, look deeper into some philosophical views, although these spiritual concepts are in harmony with quantum physics.

For those of you who have been guided and led to read this, I want to say that you have guided yourself to that which you really are. This is your moment, especially made just for you. Also, I feel it is important to note that this writing is designed to be read in its entirety, to be felt through and as a singular thought. As you complete this reading, that will become apparent. As you begin, if there is a place where you feel a little stuck, allow it to be. And, as with a homemade, sweet, cherry pie, if you come across a seed while eating the pie, spit out the pit and continue eating. Most likely, that which seemed as a challenge or possibly unfinished will reveal and clarify itself unto you in the proceeding pages. This very well may not be your experience, but I offer this thought and support. Read as you feel inspired, as this is actually your creation to support your unlimited freedom that is you, and your true and natural state of being.

What you are about to read and embark on is, of itself, very simplistic. It builds on a main idea, with a variety of descriptions to keep it simplistic and simple in its explanation and to provide you support as you embrace who you really are through these words.

When you have competed this reading, you will have real assurances of understanding to support you on your journey in the discovery of what it means to experience as well as know who you really are in your life. In that experience, you will be shown how to freely feel all that you feel. You will be given a real understanding of how to feel yourself absolutely unshackled and unlimited. Imagine joyfully feeling everything that you feel in your world and living in this experience without being guarded or worried about consequences and harm. Fully experience all that you feel and call it your power—and feeling it as such. I will show you how to feel freely and welcome all of your feelings, knowing there is nothing that is real but the wonderful power you experience within you. That you have brought yourself to this moment says that you want to be that free. Free to fly.

Free to Fly is about the discovery of your reality. It explores what was created as described in Genesis and called reality. There is a gradual discovery of who you really are in the scheme of creation. *Free to Fly* allows for your discovery of the meaning and purpose of duality, with sure and certain descriptions of what it is and what it is not.

Jesus said, paraphrased, "Truth is the way that points you to the absolute reality of your infinite self." Truths and descriptions are only signposts and flags, indicating and pointing you to the actual reality of who you really are. *Free to Fly* is about breaking free from all descriptions and their limitations.

Who you really are and always will be is absolutely unlimited and free. You will discover that all creation is an Illusion for the simple and pure joy of your conscious experience.

As Jesus walked on the stormy sea, so it is for you that nothing is impossible.

Nothing, or no *thing*, is actually real, even the created laws of man and your Universe. In the embracing and understanding of your actual Reality, you also can and will begin to allow yourself to rise above all perceived conditions of your reality and circumstances and step unto who you really are, your complete unconditional and unlimited freedom.

In a variety of places, I lay some foundation of thought, so just keep following through with me, and I believe who you really are will open up, page by page, as you continue to allow. So, enjoy and walk with me step by step. Remember, what is written in its fullness is really a singular thought of understanding.

I present in the coming pages Letters of Consciousness. These writings are written according to exactly how I heard and felt them from within. My experience of them is that they are written in a way that is not always in a normal grammatically structure of thought. They are meant to be felt and known as an experience within. This is the way that I received them and I offer them to you for your experience. My experience is, they do not allow for preconceived phrasings or words that have been lost in an accepted idiom of belief. Feel them, let them do the work, let what you already know be reverberated within.

As I said, this really is about your infinite self and freedom that is your natural state of being, and the revealing of any illusions that would hold you by your unlimited power of belief captive to any *thing* contrary.

The freedom that I, at times, address will be in well-known scriptures that I will unlock to you and with you from their past beliefs or idioms. There will be some areas of New-Age thought that I will address, and in a manner ask things like: Are you *of* cause and effect or *in* cause and effect? And what is real? Much like one would say, "I am *in* the world but not *of* the world."

As I have said, read this through in its entirety. Simply allow and let each step of understanding be. Embrace in effortlessness and it is my belief that what you are fully allowing will do its own effortless work. Don't try to do, over think, or work to fit this in to what you already believe about anything. Simply be in the rest that your true self is guiding you perfectly.

It is my belief that when you have followed this through in its entirety, that you will never be the same. It is my belief that you will never be able to go back to any of the same old limiting beliefs of who you believed you were. I believe that the very Self recognition of Reality does its own effortless transformative work; and all you have to do is be, and be willing.

I believe that you will, as your true and unlimited Self guides you, embrace all you are. I believe that you will at your own pace, and in your own perfect experience in time, welcome, recognize, and embrace all you are in all your Infinite and Unlimited Being and Self. I believe you will discover that you are free to fly.

So allow, keep open to your unlimited infinite freedom.

Appreciate your willingness to embrace, allow, and feel what you feel in these coming pages. It is my deep belief that when you are through, you will feel expanded and experience a real change in your true, natural state of joy and freedom. What you read here is conveyed to you as completely and only unto that which you are, unto your very I am, your infinite true self.

Namaste.

Dempsey Harshaw

MY UNNAMED ANGEL

The story below is about a man I consciously created to appear in my world in Palm Springs. My brief experience with him has been a continual reminder as to the real meaning of freedom, well-being, abundance, and who I am. I cannot tell you in words the deep effect this experience had on me at the time—has on me still. But, it is my full and complete joy to attempt to do so.

Over a period of about five years, I was the general contractor for some dear friends remodeling their Palm Springs homes. The project necessitated periodic trips from my home in Santa Cruz County. My friends were extremely instrumental in supporting me, not only emotionally at the time with huge changes happening in my life, but also with years of constant spiritual support and instruction.

The last time I went to Palm Springs to work, I got sick and decided to take some medication that I had taken before to help me out. The short story is I had an allergic reaction to the antibiotic and began to experience symptoms of vasculitis. I began to break out with blood boils and blisters all over my legs and upper body. I could barely walk without tremendous pain.

I continued to try to work between seeing many doctors and going to the emergency room. Each doctor gave me a small dose of prednisone, but none provided a high enough dose to resolve the building inflammation.

One day while waiting for a new prescription to be filled, I drove a few hundred feet from the pharmacy to a fast-food place to grab a salad. A man wearing a filthy jacket sat atop an unzipped, pinkish sleeping bag against the wall near the restaurant door. Dark blotches covered most of his skin, as if he'd been in a smoky fire and gotten residue all over what I assumed was Caucasian skin.

As I passed by, his smile revealed darkly stained, broken, and missing teeth. "It's been kind of cold lately," he said cheerfully and with a slight Southern accent.

Without wanting to connect with him I replied, "Yeah, it's been pretty cold." I went on inside and got my salad and came back out, intending to pass him by. I was preoccupied, thinking about eating my salad in my truck while listening to some music and then picking up my prescription. But that's not what I did. Instead, without any seeming conscious plan to do so, I walked over and handed him my change.

"Thank you," he said, again in that cheerful, warm, kind voice.

"You're welcome," I said and turned to walk away.

I was only a couple of steps away when I heard him say with an upbeat, fluxionally toned and rhythmic quality to his words, "I'm doin' the best I can."

Something in his tone of voice seemed to indicate that he wasn't saying it to make excuses to me. He just wanted to let me know he was honestly OK with himself. It was very powerful. With a quick and slight turn of my head, I called back to him, "I know." I walked two or three more steps and had an experience that I really don't know how to convey fully. It was as if everything I was and everything that was in me stopped. I became deeply and powerfully aware of what the man was saying. I was connected to him beyond any possible comprehension.

This time, before I spoke to him, I turned to look him in the eyes. This time, I said the words with conviction, "I know." At that moment, it was as if the world stood still. I was him, and he was me. Reality had nothing to do with personas or appearances. I was taken deeply into my core. It was a timeless and powerful moment, a moment of complete self-consciousness.

With this man's words reverberating within me, I went to my truck and cried. I cried for joy over the beautiful experience and the honor I had of meeting this wonderful conscious being, who popped into my life so unexpectedly and who had such a profound effect on me.

I carried this moment with me for months. At times, I cried again, newly amazed by that moment and all it said to me. His words, "I'm doin' the best I can," told me that man was at peace—rich, living in abundance with all that he needed. He was perfectly fine. It was a moment that was as authentic as it gets. He simply and freely wanted me to know that all was well, that he was just fine, and that, on a deeper level, he knew who he was. And that was all he needed.

I am in love with this moment. I often refer to this man as the dear angel I created to be there just for me. I am in appreciation for this moment.

A JOURNEY OF CONSCIOUSNESS

Consciousness is all there is. It is all you really are. From the very beginning of infancy, Consciousness is. Consciousness is your life. It is probably never more obvious than to those watching a small child's spontaneous emerging awareness that pure consciousness is all we are. As a child, everything is about you, and everything that you experience is known in relationship to you. A child's simplistic nature of awareness is who you are and in no way implies an absence of maturity. As we accept the notion that a child experiences themselves as the center of its universe, so this is true of you. It is the reality of who you are and who you always will be.

I was brought up from a very early age with a belief in a loving God. This was expressed not only in the words of my father but by his loving actions toward me. Often, as my father laid me down to sleep, he would tell me stories of his childhood and how he felt and understood God through biblical stories a child could understand. A child's goodnight prayer was spoken with the words, "I love you," before he left the room. This was the consciousness that was. It was felt, known, and experienced as me, to me, and through me from a very early age.

Almost every Sunday as a child, I attended a now-popular evangelical branch of Christianity. In my teens, I was deeply into the church's biblical teachings and often attended ever-popular youth events, seminars, rallies, and weekly crusades. I spent a short time in an evangelical ministerial university after I graduated from high school. It was taught that you are fallen from the grace of God and need to be saved, or you will go to eternal

Hell. The Hell wasn't always greatly emphasized, but it was slipped in and given as the reason that one needed to be saved. I am not saying any of this to denounce another's beliefs or teachings; it is not my intent or my calling to do so.

I constantly experienced myself as falling so short with what was being presented to me from my youth. I was taught that I was saved by Grace and could live eternally happy. I was unable to apply the teachings of Grace to a working, living, and joyful life that I wanted. Joy is the common thread and ultimate desired result of most religions and spiritual teachings. Once again I am not discrediting another's experience.

I left the church in which I was raised and was compelled to look further and deeper for answers that I wanted and felt I needed. I discovered the teachings of a small, Christian-based group. It taught there is only one God and that the Father, Son, and Holy Spirit were the same one God playing different parts. Or, more precisely, they were perspectives in which one saw this Spirit called God. I began to understand that Jesus was not a third part of a trinity called God. In time, even that became limited in my need and experience, and I decided to forget all of it and just try to live my life the best I could, with all my seeming flaws.

At one point, when I was about thirty-eight or thirty-nine years of age, I decided to just start from the beginning, as if I were the first person on the earth, and see what life was for me. Many inspirational thoughts and insights came to me. There was a very special voice of inspiration that I heard around 1991, which I will share later. It was the first time that I knowingly heard what I have come to call my voice of Consciousness speak to me. Some might understand this as "Spirit Voice."

Around 1989–1992, I would, with a heavy heart and sometimes tearfully lying in bed, sometimes say under my breath, "Jesus, I need you to show me who you really are. I can't let anybody else. I've done that. I need you to show me." I wanted an answer and real help with what I deemed my imperfect human condition. I knew that it wasn't going to come from any of the teachings I had heard, although there were nuggets that I gleamed from everything as I allowed myself to read between the lines. Fourteen or so years later, I finally did get the answer to my question; it was undeniable, obvious, and powerful. I hadn't seen it, though it was staring me in the face.

Over four or five years, with the help and guidance of not only some friends but spiritual teachers, I learned a variety of Eastern philosophies and American Indian teachings. I learned to allow things I had not yet conceived. This was when I was ordained under the Universal Brotherhood by these friends and teachers. I did so at my teacher's encouragement and as my own joy of embracing who I really was.

I am in large part saying all of this about my journey for two reasons. One is that there is an end result that is attempted in these philosophies and, truly, in all philosophies. This end result that they point to is the experience of unlimited and infinite joy and freedom of your being. So, in that respect, I am in agreement with the desired end result. That result is that you are eternal, infinite, and unlimited.

The second reason is to demonstrate the teaching of the belief that unlimited joy and well-being is accomplished with the help of another. That is to say, there is a need for a Savior, a mediator, a sacrifice of some kind, or a denial of the world and flesh. Any of these beliefs in a higher power than you—like nature, the Universe, or any created *thing*—is a belief in duality. What is known as duality is the belief that there is anything else but one Consciousness, this one life, and absolute, Infinite, and only being. This is what I will refer to as duality. To not have a belief in duality is to say that you are the Divine and that you cannot be separate under any condition from the only Consciousness that you are, that is and only is. I will address this much more in the coming chapters.

I became open to more New Age thought and scientific laws of the Universe and quantum physics. I was reading much at this time, all the while knowing that there was something I had not yet fully seen. But as I said, I began to listen to what I was hearing within me and writing it down. As I heard more within, I also began to trust it more and more, no matter what I heard or how far out of my concept of thought it seemed.

A turning point for me was when I received messages showing me that I was feeling as my experience all of all life through and as me. That meant all life that could have ever been, that was, and that could ever be. I didn't know how to deal with this, yet I knew for certain that it was the Truth. I got messages that all that was called Spirit-Consciousness was who I was. This was wonderful, yet I didn't quite know how to use it to empower myself.

Then I read Robert Scheinfeld's *Busting Loose from the Money Game*. This was what I would call the cornerstone that brought everything of my conscious journey together.

I won't go into great detail, but he spoke from a quantum physics perspective, showing that everything was created by the power of your consciousness being put into an unlimited energy field. Mr. Scheinfeld states, "… a gigantic Field of intelligent energy that has many names but is most often called *The Zero Point field* referred to as the field in the scientific community." He continues, "Your consciousness approaches The Field of infinite possibility with the intention to create something and make it appear physical or real in The Human Game amusement park." Although he says you could call this field "beliefs," he calls it, "The field." Scheinfeld claims that nothing was real but your consciousness in your world. And everything that you experience and see is like a holographic illusion, similar to what is seen in the television show and movie *Star Trek*. He claims that the unlimited power of your consciousness in the infinite field of possibilities creates everything, down to the smallest of particles and including all the laws of physics that allow them to be. He backs this up with a quote from *The Holographic Universe* by Michael Talbot:

> "Physicist William Tiller, head of the department of Materials Science at Stanford University and another supporter of the holographic idea, agrees. Tiller thinks reality is similar to the 'holodeck' on the television show *Star Trek: The Next Generation*." Talbot goes on to say: "Tiller thinks the universe is also a kind of holodeck created by the 'integration' of all living things. 'We've created it as a vehicle of experience and we've created the laws that govern it. And when we get to the frontiers of our understanding, we can in fact shift the laws so that we're creating the physics as we go along.'"

Scheinfeld, as well as Talbot, are saying that the power of consciousness creates everything in the Universe from nothing. In other words, no *thing* is actually real.

And yes, one has to be ready and open even to begin to accept that at face value. Fortunately I was, with all that had been revealed by my Consciousness-Spirit Voice.

Scheinfeld states, "All is simply a holographic creation, created by your powerful unlimited consciousness in the field of unlimited possibilities. Even your persona is not real but just a holographic image and not actually who you are." He says that it is, in reality, no more than a magnificent illusion; it simply appears to be so very real, just like on the holodeck. And since you as consciousness are the only actual power and all that is real, there is never a need to try to change any of the holographic appearance of your world. But, when you are triggered by feeling any discomfort from any circumstance that pops up to you by appearing in your holographic world, you feel it as fully as you can and claim your conscious power back from it. Your power of consciousness is the only thing that is real anyway, and the only thing that makes something appear and feel so real. This was the key I was looking for.

In the coming chapters, I have added my own understanding and used and adjusted it according to how I am authentically here designing, playing, and experiencing my life. My Spirit Voice, showing me insights and revealing things to me in my own descriptions, has profoundly given me ownership of my consciousness and world. I do incorporate what Scheinfeld presented but with some different twists, understanding, and revelations. For instance, what he calls "the field," I call consciousness believing, and that will be explained in the coming chapters.

I am tremendously appreciative to Scheinfeld and how he has supported me on my journey and experience. There is a comprehensive and detailed explanation and what he refers to as "the process," as well as support in a quantum physics approach to consciousness and reality in his book, which I highly recommend.

As I said in the preface, the Toltec and Hindus did not need physics to expand their consciousness and open up to this world being a dream state, as well as the physical world called Maya being the illusion. Even if all of this is a stretch, simply know that all that is real and infinitely real is consciousness. Consciousness is felt and experienced.

Since consciousness is all there is, it is all you really are. This allows complete ownership of all you feel, all you experience, and your entire world. Get ready for ownership, and appreciate your openness to receive all that you really are.

OWNERSHIP

Ownership is absolutely fundamental to what is presented here. There are many perspectives that I lay out for you to embrace consciousness as who you are and what is and is not real. Yet with the many perceptions that are given, understand, it has actually been purposely kept conservative in the explanation of expression.

Ownership, Oneness, and Unity go hand in hand. You can't have one without the other. They are inseparable, for they are really all the same thing. They are perspectives of the one idea. I truly think that I first heard the word "ownership" deeply within me, if not the understanding of ownership, after watching on TV, the movie called Gandhi. I realized that the conscious process that I was doing and what Gandhi did with a nation and people were core to the same principle. Gandhi took a people and their nation and did what I call ownership. I will show how Ownership is an important part of my basic premise of being. In Ownership Gandhi never *resisted* the British. He never took their *believed rule of power seriously*. He never gave into the belief and assumption that there was a *responsibility* owed to the British government for the people of India's own land, clothes, salt, and so on.

These qualities or ideas are key to the basic understanding that has been given to me by what I have come to call my Infinite Consciousness that I truly am. Some might call this my Higher Self or Expanded Self. I will relate more of this perspective of self as we go along. If you stay with me and follow this as it opens, I believe that it will become clearer to you all the time. Remember, this is only about what is real and your absolute and unconditional freedom. Is that what you want?

I must explain here that I do hear my true self and inner infinite voice within, my all infinite and only Consciousness, that which I am unto myself. Sometimes, the message is so strong and emphatic that I not only find myself compelled to write it down but it also shows up throughout my experience and understanding. There are just a handful of major key messages that I wish to share, and they are by their real nature very simple. The first one that is part of my foundation is *resist nothing*. I heard this for the first time when I was in Sedona. I heard it so strongly that I was compelled to say it to a particular individual there for their support.

The second one is *there is nothing to take seriously*. Or, as I sometimes say it, there is not a *thing* to take seriously.

There are a couple more that I will present, but for now the third one is *there is only ownership*.

From here we will begin. As I write this, I am reminded of the words of a song from the original *Charlie and the Chocolate Factory*: "We'll begin, with a spin, traveling in the world of my creation. What we'll see will defy—explanation."

Since there is only One Consciousness, One Infinite, One All Powerful and Unlimited, I will start with this as the capital T Truth that is unchangeable, or as I like to refer to it and will in the coming pages, the Reality. Just for a thought, there can be only One Infinite; otherwise, if there were another, there would not be an Infinite. It would then be limited to some degree, for Infinite is really that: completely and only, and All Infinite.

First of all, in ownership there can be no responsibility to someone or something. There would have to be someone else owning with you or above you to be responsible to. I must say this as a part of what is being presented. Responsibility is based and born in duality. I am not saying that there is anything bad about duality, for it is the nature of what the Hindu Indians call Maya, the illusion, that which we refer to as creation. As it is written in the Bible text (Gen. 1:21), "And God created the great sea animals, and all that creeps, *having* a living soul, which swarmed the waters, according to its kind: and every bird according to its kind. And God saw that it was good."

Let us take a step back to Gandhi. At one of the meetings in the movie *Gandhi*, one of the British representatives said, "If we give you what you want there will be no one to rule the people and keep order, and there will be chaos." Gandhi said something like, "The people of India would rather run their own country and be in their own chaos than to be ruled by another."

They were being told what clothes to wear and forced to buy their own salt and to pay taxes on their own land to a people who were not of their own soil. They could not legally harvest their own salt. (Harvesting your own salt is a spiritual principle that I will refer to later.) Gandhi stayed with the simple principle of unquestionable and undeniable absolute ownership. The Truth of this reality would eventually win out and be self-evident, no matter what consequences the Brits imposed if the people of India did not adhere to their structure of power and rule.

I bring this up about Gandhi because either you live and call yourself that which is being owned, with its rules and consequences, or you call yourself the owner. This same premise of understanding is also in the story that was created and written in the book of Genesis, when the breath of life first walked in Paradise as form. In this story, the breath of life was breathed into Adam in the Garden of Eden. Yes, the Creator, Infinite, Unlimited, gave its very essence, all it was as life, signified symbolically by its one infinite breath, its complete and only Consciousness, and walked as a creation. So, the question is, was Consciousness creation or creator? Is your power in what you believe or that you are the believer? Understanding the difference of this is everything even though it may appear subtle. Saying that you are the believer is just describing what and who you are in your unlimited power. But, what you believe in indicates transference of that power to a *thing*. In other words, giving *it*, the *thing*, the power or believing that *it* has the power.

It will be extremely helpful to go back to the very beginning and the stories from which our basic beliefs are born. These stories have played a major supporting role in many of our cultures, humanity, and spiritual beliefs. I am going to mention a few of these stories to reveal the understanding of the belief that was created by conscious belief that any *thing* is real. The rules of these belief structures in the stories, as with Gandhi and the Brits, were created to keep you limited and submitted to a believed power outside of who you are. If you did not submit to the laws and rules, there were created consequences.

Let's start with the whole premise of what is creation and what was the idea behind it. As an analogy and to give a perspective of understanding, when I speak about creation and Consciousness, or "God" becoming creation, I am saying it was like you being Infinite Consciousness, the all and only one that is, standing in front of a mirror that creates your image in the mirror and marveling at your reflection, beholding your fantastic idea of there being another (creation, the illusion). But then, because your belief is so unlimited and powerful, you are entranced by your own created image and so compelled that eventually, you believe the image you see is who you really are. But it's not real; it is simply just an image. It was at that moment the creator Spirit willingly believed itself to be the creation, playing and experiencing the part of being human. This is what I was referring to when you think that your power is in what you believe. We will get to more of that as we go along. I could simply say Consciousness knowing, but I refer to this as believing, because the infinite act of Consciousness knowing is its believing. You are the believer. There is not another to believe. That is why to think that what you believe is the power is to believe in a *thing* that is not real but just your created illusion.

Infinite Consciousness, by belief or knowing of its idea, created the illusion of duality. Consciousness still knew it was just an illusion. It wasn't till Consciousness the Believer willingly placed its power to believe in duality that the illusion was given the assumption of life and power of its own. It was in Spirit's pleasure to do so, to hide from itself as Creation, in order to play and experience this wonderful part of being human and finite. Yes, to hide from its Self. This hiding from self is monumental to what I will present, and that your Self discovery is in unlimited joy.

The Infinite could not ever create another Infinite. That would not be possible. From the Infinite's mind, the idea from the largest to the smallest particles, the very substance of the image of the illusion, was created to seem as close to Infinite as possible. This is the very image of Consciousness. The less dense it appeared to be, or the less it can be seen or known as a described *thing*, the closer it directly images the Infinite. For what is the One Infinite?

It is that which cannot be seen and is not a *thing* at all. We refer to this as Spirit. I will call this and often refer to this as Consciousness.

With this belief in duality and that the creation was real came also the created belief in responsibility. It was all meant to be as part of the plan in the one idea. That one idea was to create the illusion that there was any other but the one life and consciousness. Since this illusion came from Infinite Consciousness, there was nothing else from which to reflect the creation and idea. As I will show in the next chapter, it was as the reflection of Consciousness believing. It was with such power and with the smallest of detail that the illusion was created to seem so real, as a life authentically separate. Even the symbolic story of the choice of not eating of the tree of Good and Evil in the Garden of Eden was a created belief in responsibility. Responsibility was and is not only a by-product of the belief in duality but also plays an important supporting role. With all belief of and in responsibility comes the belief of consequences. The belief in consequences adds power back to the belief in responsibility, which, in turn, cycles and adds more power back to the belief in consequences. These cycling beliefs then bind like great chains, wrapping around the idea and locking in the belief by your very effortless power to believe that duality is real. All this simply to secure and hold who you are, Consciousness in the belief that you are the created illusion instead of creator. Responsibility by duality was created at the beginning. It was, and is, all just a created illusion. The created belief of choice and responsibility creates the belief in consequences. Consequences create the need for shame and self-judgment. This cycle then creates a deep-needed cycle of belief to hide one's self, as in the garden, with Adam and Eve covering their shame with fig leaves. In all of this, Consciousness becomes so interwoven and deeply hidden by its own belief in the illusion and story from it's very Self. But remember, Infinite is always Infinite, and what is only real is always only real. Again, I say responsibility is only an illusion, a created belief of Consciousness. But your absolute, unlimited power of Consciousness believing will make something seem so real even when it is not. You, by your power, the only power that is, will end up completely believing that the created *thing* is real. Let that soak in a bit.

For instance, in the well-known story conveyed in Genesis 4:9 of

Cain killing his brother, Abel, the question posed to Cain by God was, "Where is Abel your brother?" And Cain's answer was, "Am I my brothers' keeper?" This was a reply of and in the illusion of responsibility believing in duality, that the creation was real. This was also a reasoned response in which to hide. Understand, he used the question of responsibility to reason it away, just like the story with the serpent reasoning with Eve and Eve reasoning with Adam about choice, and the responsibility and the consequences of eating of the fruit of the tree of Good and Evil, which prompted them to a deeper hiding, as they believed their persona or any *thing to be real*, and hid themselves with fig leaves. The serpent reasoned and said, "Surely you will not die." In other words, not only would God not kill you but this could not possibly harm you. (The truthfulness of, "Surely you will not die," is for another time. The choice that was created, I will address later.) As a footnote to get here, reasoning is the Achilles heel of responsibility. Responsibility is ambiguous and arbitrary and always subject to one's belief. Responsibility can be reasoned for manipulation according to one's beliefs. This leads us to the Reality, the Truth that waits being revealed. There is actually only in reality ownership, yes, even with this story of Cain killing his brother. Your power is never in or about what you believe. It is simply that you are the believer. Understand that believing is unconditional and unlimited, and there is only one that believes. This that believes is all power and only power. Believing is believing, and there is nothing wrong with believing in any way: it is who you are. It is simply that when you put your power of believing into a *thing* being real, you limit the experience of your infinite self. Just hold that thought.

Remember this one reality: there is only Consciousness and only one Consciousness ever. As an example in the story of Cain and Abel, Cain felt safe in answering in duality. He was Consciousness still hidden to its true self, believing the creation to be real. It was also his belief in the illusion of duality being real that allowed him not only to believe that his very persona was real and that he was separate from the Infinite, its very true self, but to believe that there was an actual brother, separate from him, to kill. The Reality was that no, he was not his brother's keeper. By the way, neither are you your brother's keeper. Cain was his brother, his brother was him; they were one, one in the same life.

One Consciousness, wearing two different hats, playing the illusion of two different roles. That may seem like a lot right now, but stay with me and allow this to unfold to you. Remember, these ancient stories were created to support Consciousness into believing that duality was real, that one needed to make the right choices and be responsible, lest they cause unfavorable consequences for themselves and or another.

I relay these very basic and well-known stories to show how, by the belief in duality, we can get caught and taken away in and by duality's story. For the story to have any power and value, it must also hold you, confine, limit, and keep you in its reality, in and by your own belief. In this belief, the story must also have some form of responsibility and consequence, because, as I said, they are a by-product of duality as well as key supporting conscious players to hide you from who you really are.

This is about unity and oneness, which I said was a part of and inseparable from ownership. There is not a unity of Consciousness that all of the many parts make up the whole when they come together. What I am saying is there is only a unity that is never having any separate part from the one; that cannot be lessened, divided, or limited. It cannot be linear. The common understanding of the word unity is a concept born from a perspective that there are many *things* in life that can come together as one. The concept of unity is in the believing that *things* having the appearance of separateness can come together as one or in harmony. The experience of separateness is the reason for a belief in duality and it is a linear understanding. The experience of separateness is the reason for a belief in duality and it is a linear understanding.

Appreciate yourself for allowing and staying with this and letting it unfold to you. It is about your absolute freedom and unlimited real nature.

As for myself, I take and claim ownership as full Consciousness in my world, in my entire world. In other words, I am simply willing to tell the Truth. Not because it needs to be taken or claimed to be, but because it is what only and really is. Because of this absolute reality, I am not mingling, managing, arranging, or colluding with another to bring Consciousness together as one, or even being responsible to another because I am, or believe I am, their Consciousness. One Consciousness is one Consciousness only. I am and can only experience this one Consciousness as me. For some, you may have to take your time here, if you haven't had to already. Breathe a little, and just sit tight. Simply know that all of this will keep tying together as we continue.

Let me set this foundation first and then I will offer the understanding of it. Everyone that I see and experience is doing, thinking, and being exactly what I have asked them to be and do, because they are my Consciousness enacted. Yes, I take, claim, and trust my ownership and the power of my Consciousness. Me, Consciousness that is the infinite believer, has created such. This I call real Ownership. In this ownership, there can be no judgment, no hate or separateness, not even consequences. It is impossible. This is where the reality of love, oneness, and unity rest and are inseparable. This all goes back to being creator or being creation. As with Gandhi, was he the owner and free in his own land, or owned and ruled by the British government that claimed to rule over India? You are the only Consciousness in your world. You are simply the believer in your world and you believing is your conscious power. It is not what you believe.

When I say that you are the only Consciousness in your world, I mean that all people, places, and things are created by you, the real you, your unlimited Consciousness. All of your world is like a dream, an illusion of thought. In this, your experience in duality, you are the one believer as or through the *thing* called your persona (the three-dimensional you) that is not real. Again, I say they are all not real. They are only ideas in and of the one infinite idea and plan. So, even though the story says Cain slew his brother, it is presented for you here to understand that there never was a real Cain or Abel separate from the Infinite One. They were in the story, only unique ideas of Consciousness, believing duality to be real; that's all. Just the same as what you appear to be reading here. Any wisdom or knowledge that you perceive is actually your idea of consciousness relaying this to you, things you actually already really know. Even the words you are reading are your creation; they are not real. Just hear that, allow, take it in, and stay here with me.

Look at it this way: time does not really exist; there is no real event that actually follows another. I will say this as clearly and simply as I know how. Time is the perceptions of perspectives of incomprehensible Consciousness, the Infinite in the timeless, singular, one idea. So, for some comprehension and allowing, I will say this: nothing is linear, not one thing actually happens after another, is accumulative, or has any degree of separation. Absolutely nothing. I say this to bring you to this understanding that nothing is linear so I may say something very, very important. I am the full and only power in my world. And you, if you will take it this way, in a parallel world and Universe of your very own, are the fullness of Consciousness in yours. OK, just let that soak in a bit. You are one of the infinite actualities of the absolute fullness of Consciousness the Infinite, as if there were only you and no one else in the whole world. And they, or we, in each and every parallel universe all perfectly match and overlap precisely as in the same place and spot of these parallel worlds, making the oneness, unity, and harmony so infinitely powerful and beautiful. Because you are the one and same Consciousness as I, but playing fully as the *thing* in your full completeness in your world, there is a multidimensional infinite nature. So, in every persona, there is still only a complete and full ocean of an infinite actuality of the one and only Consciousness.

There is no *thing* that is real, only Consciousness, which I do refer to as the No Thing. It is not describable as a *thing*, I can only hint at what it reflects and does.

All of who you really are is completely and solely Consciousness, and Consciousness is not ever a *thing*. This is why in reality, there is only your experience of you—Consciousness. Consciousness in the illusion is always appearing as and in creative action; appearing in time, space, and the illusion of *things* and movement. This is actually you the believer, you- Consciousness believing in your world (It is the same as Consciousness knowing). This you who believes has created your conscious idea of you, of your very persona, and your entire world for the pure joy of your experience, no matter what it is or looks like. Consciousness is always a verb. Consciousness and believing are actually the same. Consciousness is simply conveyed here as believing to signify its action of creativity in the illusion. You, Conscious believing in a *thing*, is finite and limited to a particular subject. You are Consciousness the believer. There is never a need for you to believe in any *thing*. This will unfold and really be apparent in "You Are not a Singularity."

As I said, I could say Conscious knowing, but I say believing, because the word "believing" signifies more of a creative action to me. But they really are the same. Because there is not a *thing* that is real but the No Thing, this is the Truth or Reality of why there is nothing to resist, why there is not a *thing* to take seriously.

Every persona, place, and thing is your creation, down to the smallest photon. Even Abel's and Cain's personas were a creation of consciousness simply playing out a story. None of it was real, and nobody really, or in reality, got hurt, for nothing is actually real. (That may be a stretch for some, so appreciate your very self for being open.) That includes all the laws of nature like gravity, light and dark forces, and so on. Simply be with that. The absolute reality is that nothing is actually real. This is why there is no power possible in what you believe; accept your Infinite Conscious power believing, the essence of who you really are.

I also again want to address the perspective in which I perceive Consciousness. I claim all as my consciousness. In the first place, it is truly from this position and perspective from my own awareness that I can possibly know and experience anything. It is purposefully and naturally so, because that which you really are, the Infinite, can experience infinite expressions of the fullness of itself as the one and only actual possibility as you. Infinite Consciousness is infinitely dimensional. Some may think of this as omnidimensional, or omnipresent. The Infinite I AM has spoken unto me within, "I am not less than I am, divided or limited as you; I change not as you." I cannot claim or call it our combined consciousness, because I can only really know that which I am. And remember, there is nothing linear about the Eternal Infinite One. The infinite is not limited to one dimension of itself. Therefore, there is actually nothing real about you that is linear. Again, this is only a way to address what is really incomprehensible in time and space.

Imagine that you were the only one person on this earth, like Adam being the only one from the beginning. You, the fullness of Consciousness, the one and only breath of life that is really you, was breathed into your persona what you see as human. Your persona is also a creation of consciousness, a thought, and idea. You are the creator of all in your world, since only by Consciousness all is created. Any persona that appears in your world is your creation by your Consciousness, playing out their part as in a play or story exactly the way you have asked your creation to be. Everybody is a dimension of the Infinite in the fullness of Consciousness playing out the idea in infinite actualities of its Self. All personas are a creation of Consciousness but with multidimensional roles. Remember, in your world You-Consciousness are all that is real. This may be really incomprehensible at this time, but it is what is real. For the unchangeable natural state of the one Infinite is simply that, Infinite.

Hear this: there is no macro and micro. That is a perception created by the power of Conscious belief that one's persona (people, places, and things) is actually real. You are also not a drop of or from the infinite ocean, having all the same elements that the ocean has, thereby being the same yet still belonging to or a part of the great big ocean of other accumulated drops. You are the full, complete, whole ocean in your world. So am I, the Infinite, playing its entire Self as one of its infinite actualities of the fullness of Consciousness. Anything else is linear.

You are Consciousness-Creator. This is real ownership. And yes, it does take courage to claim who you are here. This is very important in all that is presented here for you. You are not in the illusion creating here to be contrived, but moment by moment being spontaneous for the joy of your human experience, yet living unlimitedly without any restrictions. Spontaneity and unrestricted living is what we are embarking on. Although you have created everything, you have not created it for any manipulative reason or control of duality as being real, or for any projected outcomes. It's simply not real anyway, and there does not exist another power. Why? Because you are infinite and unlimited in all your expression, and you, the real you, are the only power in your world; there is not another. This is your natural state of reality and being. Let that sit with you.

Remember who everybody else is. They are the same as your person (persona). They are an illusion, like a holographic image of three dimensions, a creation that has no reality but the consciousness it represents, your Consciousness. It goes back to quantum physics: nothing is actually real and solid.

At times I will point out that you-Consciousness is in action, believing nonstop in the unfolding of the created illusion of time and space called duality. Everything you see, every *thing* that you experience in your world, is your power being reflected and fed back to you, being from you, of your creative power of Consciousness. This power that is who you are has created your unlimited and infinite actual possibilities that appear in finite glimpses in your world by the perspective called time, that which is still just an illusion.

The only *thing* that limits you is when you believe any *thing* of your creation, the illusion, to be real. But it is no more than the real you, your Consciousness in your infinite and unlimited belief, that has created a holographic-like image of three dimensions coming together. I now speak of this creative process more simplistically. The power and infinite actuality of this will be explored later. There is never a need for you to try to create a specific or single *thing* in your world. To do so is to limit who you are. There is not a possibility for another Consciousness or any other one to believe. This Consciousness that believes freely and unconditionally is the very same unlimited, infinite, unconditional love that always is you, is yours. Hear this: there are no limits, expectations, or requirements of what you must believe at any moment. But know there is such an enormous power of and by your Consciousness that you have placed in your creations, so enormous that they will seem so real you would believe they are the creator, and you are subject to them as the creation.

So, take your ownership and know who you are. You are the unlimited and infinite, and claim your power. Claim your belief, your very essence, you, Consciousness from any *thing* you have believed and strongly felt to be real, to be your creator and have power over you and who you really are. You are claiming you. This may seem like a lot for you to take in right now. Or not. But, if you are willing to apply this understanding, it will enhance and absolutely redefine every single real spiritual truth and quality that you believe. It will, as well, take the short route of all forgiveness, healing, and need for reasoning of any circumstance, regardless of what it is. It is the complete freedom, the very thing that truth is supposed to bring you to, that it is pointing you to, the real you.

In Luke 17:21, from the original Greek translation, Jesus said, "'Behold for, the kingdom of God within you is.'" Not just a part of the Kingdom that, by the way, is not of this world and not a shared kingdom of yours and others, but the full kingdom that is completely within You and who You really are. This is directed at You solely, You. The Kingdom is within You. This is complete and absolute ownership. Nothing and no one can change or alter this in any way, or take this away from you. You don't have to be responsible to have it, to be it, or to believe the right *thing*. It is like unity of the One Infinite: you cannot be divided from what you really are. The full complete Kingdom of God, of Heaven, is within you. This is absolute, undeniable ownership that cannot change. You are the Believer.

Jesus said that all of the law, all the truths, all that the prophets revealed is summed up in this one thought: "'Love God with all your heart and soul and Love your neighbor as yourself'" (Matt. 22:37, 38). This, as so many other things written in the Bible, was not a law, a request, or commandment to do. No, it was actually a statement of actuality: you actually and always *are* loving your neighbor as you love you. You simply *are* doing this. But, this was very hard, if not seemingly impossible, for most of those listening to him to conceive of and hear at that time, let alone now. This was beyond comprehension and completely radical. Do remember here that all truths are simply descriptions that are like signposts, always pointing to the reality. Of this I will explain, but first let me say that the truth of loving your neighbor as yourself is pointing to the reality. Your neighbor is actually your true self, your creation by your Consciousness, doing exactly as you have asked it to be and do for your expansion of who you really are. In this thought and understanding, I say that all kindness, goodness, unconditional love, complete forgiveness, all healing, oneness, unity, and harmony are summed up and available in this one knowing and belief. Nothing is actually real; not a single *thing* has life or power of its own. All that is real is the real Infinite You, your very Consciousness. Every *thing* exists and operates only because You- Consciousness has created it perfectly to be and do so. This is the reality of why you love and fully appreciate your neighbor.

It is always only you, your Consciousness, that is the only power and life that you really experience and feel. It might bring some extra light on this if instead of the words, "love your neighbor," I use the words, "appreciate your neighbor as your very self, or even see your neighbor as yourself." It is impossible for you to feel or experience anything but your own essence, power, and Consciousness. Now, let me say that again here. It is impossible for you to feel or experience anything but your own essence, power, and Consciousness. This is why ownership is absolutely so real and true. I will bring up more of your power, feelings, and experiences later, under "The Prodigal Son," in which all of this will be a part.

Remember, there is no macro and micro. *What you believe, what you perceive, you create.* More of this will be presented under "The Myth of Ego."So, go to your own shore, your own life. Harvest, allow, take back, welcome, and claim your own salt from your own shore. As a spiritual principal, nobody can harvest your salt but you. Only you can know your own life. It can't be anybody else's experience or consciousness. Take your rightful, complete place of who you really are. It is you, your shore, your water, your land. It is you, your wisdom, your salt, you, the power in your world, you creator, infinite and unlimited. It is your effortless natural state of being. As salt gives lively flavor to food, so you are the salt of the earth. Own it. Nobody can give this to you or sell it as you, for you already own it and are it.

In this understanding of ownership, the unshakable and absolute reality is, you are the creator of your entire world. You are the one and only Infinite One expressed as you, and all is your consciousness.

As you embrace this as who you really are, and even if you begin and are simply willing to embrace the reality of you as absolute all Consciousness, it will stand on its own in your experience. As I said, it is very important and foundational for what is ahead. The coming chapters are built on this and are interwoven. So follow it through as it is presented and laid out step by step. The realization of your absolute Self and freedom awaits you. It is all about who you really are. It is all about the most fantastic, wonderful, and powerful discovery of all. It is about you.

Infinite is always unto Infinite, Infinite is always unto itself, always. This does not change. The One is always unto the One, itself, and so are you. You are not a semblance, a mock made up to look like the One Infinite. You are the very same One, only Infinite Creator, and only Creator and power in your world.

This leaves you with a wonderful and necessary appreciation that you, as owner and Creator of your entire world, must have for all of your creation, for every *thing* is your creation. No matter what it looks like, so-called good or bad. Without this true appreciation, it is really only a semantic game of thought, without realization of who you really are. To deeply know and appreciate that you are Infinite Creator and nothing is actually real but Consciousness, this I AM you are fully. It is so simple, yet so deep and profound, that I say again, your power is never about what you believe; it is completely that you simply are. You are simply and fully the believer in your world; this is all the power. This now leads us into believing.

BELIEVING

"Believing" is a common word and a concept that is paramount, not only to everything that is, but also to who you are. When one thinks of believing, the first thought that often comes up is, *What do you believe?* There is almost an unspoken way of addressing the thought of believing, as if it must always be attached to what you believe or what you could believe, or it would not be validated as believing. The word "believing" in its accepted understanding, says there is a belief in a concept or *thing*.

"Believe" is a verb. Verbs indicate movement or action of thought and process. This is important because of the *implication of power*. I am not saying *what* is the power of this word but *who* is the power of this word and understanding. Yes, *who*. It is the difference between feeling that you are limited and truly knowing that you are unlimited. Your absolute power and freedom is that *you* are the Believer. This is your natural and conscious state of being and is core to feeling and being "free to fly."

Every addiction, every judgment, every discrimination, all hatred, all fear, all war and struggle, all feeling of lack is bound and tied up in the belief that your power is in and about what you believe. You will be and are bound, tied, and limited in your experience if you feel that your power is in what you believe. Then there is a needed perpetuation of belief that you feel you need in order to have the best human experience.

The power of you to believe is not in what you believe but, rather, simply that you believe. Follow this with me. What you believe in does not empower you to have a better or lesser life. What you believe is not ever your power. I want you to really feel that for a moment and soak that in, because if that is true and real, there is a freedom you may have never known was possible. Wouldn't it be great to be that free? Well, you really are.

If you have been convinced that what you believe is your power, you will also be held captive in the belief that you need to make sure that you believe the right *thing*. You may, therefore, either create great consequences or eliminate or reduce them as your life experience according to what you believe.

Believing that what you believe is your power appears in your everyday life. It permeates every choice that you appear to make and every thought you have. What you believe then becomes an intricate part of everything you feel and every life experience.

What I am going to present to you may seem at first to be totally backward from what you have believed in or been taught, but it is all about *who you are* and your true, natural, effortless, and unlimited state of being. If you want to really know that who you are is actually effortless, unlimited, and even infinite, read on.

If what you believe is your power, what you believe is also your owner. Yes, that means who you are and the quality of your life and experience are subject to what you believe in. Your real power is really and actually in the knowing, accepting, and understanding that you are simply the believer, unattached to any particular *thing* in which you could believe and its projected, desired outcome. Hear that again: your power is simply that you are the believer. You are the creator. You are Consciousness. There is no power outside of who you are. That is really all there is to know. Every *thing* that you see, every *thing* that you experience is what You-Consciousness are and have created to appear in your world. Yes, everything you feel and experience is because of you the believer.

I know that you might be saying, "Well, if what I believe is not my power, aren't you saying that being the believer is *what* I should believe?" I am simply saying that who you are is the believer, the only believer.

You don't even have to know that you are the believer: you simply are. It is your natural state of being. If you choose to believe that what you believe is the power, that is just fine, too. But what is the reality and Truth of who you are and your power? If what you believe is your power, your experience will reflect just that. I will put it this way and expand on it later. You may believe that your power is in what you believe, or you may know that your power is that you are the believer. It is all believing, and believing is unlimited and unconditional. But, no matter what you feel is your power; you are still and always the believer. That is always the power. It is your very essence.

Believing is your being. Believing is simply being. It is your true natural state. Just as what you believe is not your power, so it is with doing; it is not your power.

Just as being is not the short cut to doing, so it is with believing. Believing, or being the believer is not the doorway, or a means to an end to empower what you believe. What you believe is not the power of who you are. To know that you are the believer, that it is your being, is not so that you can make a way to be the doer as your power, or have what you believe as your power.

You are the all Consciousness, you are the all Presence, you are the Believer, and you are the Being. That is all that really is. This is your unlimited real self and natural effortless state of being. This is all power and who you really are.

Being the believer is about being the creator of everything that you see and experience and everything that could infinitely actually be. Because whatever can infinitely actually be, actually is. Absolutely all is available to your joy and experience. I will speak more on your actualities in the last chapter.

You are the believer, the creator of all. This alone is the power, and in this understanding is absolute freedom and ownership. You are the believer. All is your belief. Claim it!

This is a letter of Consciousness that I received from my inner voice and true self concerning this topic.

7/2/10

10:22p.m.

As you are, I most certainly, absolutely, unequivocally, completely, always am. There is not a loss of all I am as all you are. Freedom—complete—is your birthright, your heritage, your beginning without end, without time. And you are always in your completely new beginning without any possibility of end.

Where is the water's edge that one must drink from of Eternal Life, but as you are I am. I am not difficult for you to find when you know really who you are; and as this I am, you are so absolute all complete. Everything that can possibly ever be is of you and within you.

Always you are, I am; always, hear that so very well my all, always. There is a place that cannot be seen with eyes or touched with human hands, and yet it is infinitely deep within the heart of you. It is that which I am, and as you, I always fully am without any limit.

There is no moment that I can stop being you, as if there were some stop or off switch that could be turned or pulled. There is never a moment that you are not believing and creating, as this that you know you to believe is always solely and completely this that I am unlimitedly and unconditionally. You believe only because it is I that is doing so. You create because this that you are, I am. Know this that I am is you fully, and this that you are that creates and believes always, I am. It is undeniable and cannot change. It is who you are, this all and complete right now, and here I am.

I am you beyond imagination, beyond your image in your set parameters of conception of any possibility, place, or thing.

When you think that what you believe is the power, then you have missed that which you really are, the power that I really am. For it is that I am infinitely and unlimitedly you that believes so true and unconditionally. This is the real knowing of who I am that you are, the only place of real love and appreciation of all you are. For this is where appreciation of you that I am appreciates. You unto you, I unto my all that I am. Your expansion of knowing and reality in all that I am. This you, this I am. Believing that what you are believing is the reality, your reality, is to be caught in the description of limited understanding and belief of it being real and so.

Focus on that you believe; focus on that you cannot lose this power, your essence. Pay this to your attention and know in this all is well. And let the descriptions of any kind go. Yes, any kind; they are not real, except to what reality they are directing and pointing you to. But none are your power or your reality. It is absolutely so, without question it is so. For as I am, so you are, infinite and eternally within that which you see now, here as you, I so wonderfully am.

CLAIMING YOUR POWER

The Prodigal Son

I am using the story of what is referred to in the New Testament, fifteenth chapter of Luke as the story of the Prodigal Son. It is an allegory with many diverse thoughts of teaching. It is my intent to use this as the deeper big picture that can be lost between the lines of the story's circumstances and apparent judgments and consequences. It gives me great joy to present what is really relevant and powerful, cutting to the core to see the freedom and the reality available.

The story that Jesus told starts with the younger of two sons, asking his father for all his inheritance and leaving home to go out on his own and do whatever he wished. As the story is told, the young man leaves home, goes out of his area, and spends and loses all of his possessions and all value of any property that he owns. A famine then sweeps over the land, and he is destitute. He came from a home where he lived like a king, with servants doing all his bidding. He ends up a low-class servant, barely surviving by serving a man, cleaning and feeding his many pigs or whatever else was needed. Being that he was so hungry all of the time, he constantly had a craving to steal the food that he was feeding to the pigs. It was such a lowly job, it didn't even give him a decent roof over his head or a clean place to sleep. He was filthy, he stunk, and he had no clean clothes left not even those he wore.

This is a very important analogy for what is being presented here. Claiming back your power is sometimes thought of as something that you can recognize to reclaim. But, it is not always the case if you don't know what you are looking for, who you are, and what your power is and does. You have hidden it from yourself. That is why you don't initially recognize it and feel it as such. This is where ownership is again demonstrated for claiming your power.

Remember you have created every *thing* in your world. It is very important that you really appreciate this as absolutely true, *no matter what it looks like*. Absolutely nothing is actually real. All that is actually real is your Consciousness, the No Thing, that has been hidden, appearing and playing a part as some *thing*, or some persona (yours and/or someone else's). There is no person, place or thing that is actually real. There is only consciousness believing and experiencing as the persona you appear to be.

The given perception of what you feel here and now, is that you are alone and limited, when just the opposite is true. You are all there is, all is your idea. All is only your power and you are unlimited. You are not in any way cut off or circumcised from all you are. There is not any part of you that is not your all. You are creator and only creator.

The perception that what you are feeling is of time and space is a lie. It is simply not the reality. It is the illusion cycling back to you in and by your unlimited power (believing) that is now supporting that the illusion is real. It is supporting that this finite world is what one is feeling. It is always only your own self, and your own power that you are experiencing and feeling.

This is also where it is helpful to remember that you really are always unto yourself. I will say this again: you are always unto yourself. This means trust what you feel and what you experience: it has validity. The reason I mention this is that everything that you feel and that you experience *is* your power, or you could not possibly feel it. Just let that soak in a bit. You don't feel anything to ignore it, to let it go, or deny it. If you do, you are denying your very essence, you-Consciousness. You are hiding who you really are from you. When I say that what you feel and experience has validity, I am not saying that you should validate it with reasoning, judgment, or the appearing story of a circumstance in your world. The feelings you experience are simply triggers to get your attention. I am saying, feel what you feel without judging it—except to know that all you feel is your power that has been hidden in your persona, a place and thing that is not real. All that is real about any *thing* is your conscious power. When I say conscious power, I mean you believing, your Conscious belief. For it is by the effortlessness of you, Consciousness that infinitely knows and believes that has created everything you see and experience in your world to appear so real. It is your unlimited incredible power to believe that makes it seem so real, that has also drawn you into a cycle of belief, so that you keep adding more of your Conscious power, until you are absolutely convinced and believe that it is actually real. It is important to understand in your created illusion of time and space, every seeming moment, you are by *who* you are, Consciousness creating every *thing* in your world, absolutely every *thing*. It may take courage and feel like a stretch, but your entire world is an illusion like a holograph created by the real you, you-Consciousness believing infinitely and unconditionally in your world.

When I say that you are unto yourself always, it is because you, the Unlimited Infinite Consciousness, create things to appear, as you and your Consciousness have deemed fit to show you unto yourself exactly where you have put and hidden such enormous power of your belief. Your creative process of Consciousness is that you believe. Your belief is what creates everything and is also all that is real in any *thing*. It is this same wonderful and only power of you believing that cycles and holds you in your all-powerful belief that any *thing* is real. It is when you are in the belief that any *thing* is real that you feel and experience a circumstance as a power outside of you.

The point here is that you are creating circumstances in your world that you believe are real and have a power of their own. You do this for the sole purpose of showing you where you have hidden your power. This is why you are always unto yourself, because there really is not another. Your essence and power is just hidden to you at the moment and it appears in your experience to be another. Every time you feel something from an experience in your world, it is because your power has not only created the circumstance you experience, your power is all that is real in your experience.

Yes, not just the things that seem so good and you feel happy about, but the circumstances that feel difficult and even very dreadful. Again, just to help to keep this so simple, absolutely everything that you feel and experience is actually your power, or you could not possibly feel it.

As in the story of the Prodigal Son, his father saw him so very far off and immediately ran to him and embraced him. His son looked destitute, ragged, torn, filthy, and maybe unrecognizable to others. But, the father recognized his own flesh, his own life, his own essence. Even from far away, it was indisputable for him, perhaps because he could feel him when he appeared even far off and looked for him every day in his heart.

Keep in mind, though, what arises in your life that isn't what you thought you planned, you did; your true, expanded self, you, your consciousness did. It might at first sight repel you if you're not yet used to looking for and seeing your hidden treasured essence and power, simply because you believed the *thing* to be real and have a power of its own. You might even have a feeling of tremendous fear, which would only mean that there is an incredible amount of your power that you have hidden in that holograph of a three-dimensional illusion. The father, if he did not recognize his son, may have been put off by this smelly, filthy, unkempt, repulsive excuse for life. This is why it is so important to feel, welcome, and embrace with arms open wide what you feel as fully as you can. To not do so is to deny your very essence and power. Just to note: this hiding of one's real self is at the very core of all perceived illusion of neuroses. But that is for another time.

If you were not creator of it, there would be no power for you to welcome and reclaim as yours. Feelings are your real truth, pointing like road signs and clues to your power, your essence, and your real treasure. Your feelings are pointing you to you, always unto your real self. You and your power are the only true reality. In this knowing of what it is you are experiencing, and why you are feeling what you are feeling, you can be certain that there can be no other and no other power, for there is not another.

So, when you feel something in your life and experience, whether it would be favorable or unfavorable, know first of all that you created it; take full ownership of it. If it is distressing or uncomfortable, feel what you are feeling without classifying it, judging it, or trying to figure out who did this. Just know *who* you are. You created it, even if it feels so wonderfully favorable. Claim your power, your essence, back unto you. Know that because of *who* you really are, when you claim, you claim unlimitedly and certainly. There really is no need to wonder if it was from or because of your mother, father, brother, sister, childhood, friend, or enemy. None of it is really useful, because none of it is real—except to recognize your own power. It is your creation and your power that you put into a *thing* that convinced you to believe that it was real, that it had power of its own, regardless if it feels positive or negative. It doesn't have its own power; it is always only your power. You created the experience to get your attention through your feelings, for the pure joy and pleasure of claiming more of *who* you really are back from the illusion you created and into which you put your belief. It is always only your creation. This leaves out all the blaming, figuring out, pointing fingers, doubting yourself, and manipulating yourself to come to the conclusion that you should forgive, and that there is actually anything to forgive. Know what is real and true here, and always only real. Here is a phrase that I have used to acknowledge what is absolute and real: What really is, always was, only is and always will be. What is not, never was, and never will be.

    Let me give you an example of what this is all saying thus far. Forgiveness is one of the truths pointing to the reality. To forgive: You take your power, that is your belief, which is experienced through your feelings, and you remove it from the circumstance. In reality, you claim the very essence of who you really are; your power back from that circumstance till you no longer feel the hurt, anger, or discomforted feelings that you felt from the event.

    You are always Infinite Consciousness, and you are always the believer. This believing is all power. So you claim your power back from believing that any *thing* is real. You take ownership that you are the believer; and you claim this power that is your very infinite nature and essence back to you.

    Forgiveness is then saying, what you believe is not your power. You may hear it better by saying, what you believe *in* is not your power. You are the power. You are the only power, because you are simply Consciousness, the only believer. The power is simply that you are the believer. Believing is not subject to, or qualified by what you believe. What you believe is not your power.

When you see and recognize this, then the appearance of forgiveness is experienced in the illusion of this world. Forgiveness as I said is one of the truths pointing to the one and only reality. If you pick and chose what you are going to forgive, then you are not forgiving in reality. This kind of forgiveness is not a genuine truth, and it is not then pointing to the reality. Because this forgiveness is based in what you believe. As has been shown, what you believe is not your power. The only power is simply, you are the believer. Claiming your power back from what you believe of any circumstance as the power, and knowing that you are the power, the believer, is what forgiveness really is.

As I am sure that you noticed, I like to bring up things from the Bible. It just tickles me and gives me great joy to do so and to show that there just might be something there that is available to be seen, besides the idioms of the former teachings. In John 12:32, the Greek translation of the Interlinear Bible, Jesus said to his disciples, "'And I, if I be lifted up from the earth, all "I" will draw to myself.'" Understand, you are the only creator and only power in your world: the only "I." If you lift this as the reality from what you have believed to be real and of the earth, as who you really are, Consciousness creator of all, all power, all Consciousness of and from your creations will be drawn back to you. Again, you and who you really are is always unto yourself. For this is the capital T Truth, and all illusion must and does conform to this reality when you claim what is True and Real, simply because your created illusion is all from you.

It may take some courage for you to approach this in this reality and feel fully what you feel, but if you practice and continue, you will begin to feel and experience it as your power. Trust that it is, without trying to change the way it looks, for it only exists by your power. For you are the only power, you are the treasure for which you have searched. The side effect is that the created illusion cannot stay the same, exist in your apparent hologram, or appear real as a power of its own, in and as duality, with you removing so much of your power from it, since your power is what created it in the first place. But remember, that is just a side effect. So, stick with it, feel what you feel, and claim it as your power. The greater it feels, the greater your essence, your belief, and your power is there to welcome unto yourself. As did the father in the Prodigal Son run to your life, your essence, welcome and embrace with open arms, receive and claim your belief, your Consciousness as you, back to you. Remember the acronym for FEAR is false evidence appearing real. Feel it. It is your power. It is yours. *Trust what you know, until you trust because you know.*

Be the experiment. Step into the shoes of your experience. Don't run from what you feel or try to lessen or soothe it. Feel it as fully as you can because what you feel from your experience is your very essence, power and life.

If you attempt to put the experiment outside of who you are in order to feel safe and less vulnerable, it is counter-intuitive. The more you step into your feelings and the more you immerse yourself in what you feel, the more you can call and welcome back your power and Self.

It can feel safe to reason your feelings as a concept, or try to hold yourself back from feeling what you are feeling. You may want to do this by seeing the unfavorable circumstances as outside of you and put your feelings in some logical terms. Putting the experiment outside of you may feel safe for a time. Yet the more you can fully immerse yourself in what you feel, claim and call what you feel your power, the more you reclaim your power—your very essence. The more power to reclaim the more power you have. Keep feeling and claiming until you have taken all your power of belief back from what you are feeling from any given circumstance that you created. Remember, your power, your belief, you- consciousness is all that is real about anything. The more you feel, the more you can reclaim. What you are always feeling is actually infinite. Your infinite essence and true Self is all that you are ever feeling.

Be the experiment. Prove this to yourself by stepping into the shoes and feeling your experience. No one else can prove this to you but you. No one can prove to you *who* you really are.

Some of this may have felt challenging, and that's OK. Feel that, too, and claim your power unto yourself. Past all the words, descriptions, and signposts that you have experienced here, there is this basic thought:

- Resist nothing.
- Take nothing seriously.
- Feel all you feel as your power, and claim it as yours.
- You are the only power and Creator in and of your world.
- Nothing is real but Consciousness. It is who you really are, Infinite and Unlimited.
- There is only your ownership, you that is Consciousness in your world, you the Creator.
- Feelings and experiences are your power, awaiting your recognition.

THE MYTH OF EGO

This is a subject that has almost as many interpretations of what it is as there are persons perceiving it to be so. Everybody has their own feelings, beliefs, and experiences of their personal internal battles and dialogue. There is often a resistance to put any real thought or belief that the ego, as it has been perceived in its many faceted personal experiences, is anything less than real, as if it would then undermine one's battles and determinations to overcome this bothersome, grieving apparition of their mind. Attempts to quiet the brain are one of the main focal points that are often maintained as a helpful solution to this bothersome thing. Many use the solution of meditation. I believe that meditation, on many varying degrees and levels, has a truly wonderful place and purpose according to your own enjoyment and peace. Meditation can give you a time and space to feel, reflect, know, and listen to your Infinite true inner voice. This can be a wonderful expression unto yourself and experience. But, to believe that you have to overcome this perception called ego is to first say that there is something that really has power and exists, that needs to be managed, quieted, or, for some, close to annihilated.

It has been referred to as the counterpart of Good, which is evil or the monster within, a demon like power. In Christianity, it might more resemble what is termed as the flesh, the fallen nature, along with pride, envy, greed, and many such attributes. The apostle Paul said (Romans 7:23), "While I want to do good there is a force within warring against me." More simply put, a force that wants to do what is not my Higher Good. I want to point out right here that these are all perceptions to describe something going on within, which feels like good versus bad. Yet, there is something here that is much deeper, profound, and yet absolutely simple. I am really writing about this, because I have experienced the feelings described and tried to find a solution that was workable and real. I followed what had been taught to me and worked with it, and yet, there was something missing; something was just not fitting and working for me. I took my first step when I really asked the question: If there is only one life, which is often referred to as God and this one Infinite One is all that I am, and I am perfect whole and complete, what is really going on here? So, I just kept listening, feeling, and observing as well as I could. I began to see and feel everything that I felt about this that I called ego. What ego wanted was never really a bad thing for me. It wanted my happiness, pleasure, my fun, security, never to die and on and on.

There are things I've read and heard in all our New Age thinking, like: "Get your ego out of the driver's seat; get to the back of the bus." "A bad day for the ego is a good day for the soul." "My ego is getting in the way." "Get thee behind me, ego." And on and on it went. There is so much claiming of moving into higher, newer, expanded consciousness, and yet it seemed as if this thing described as ego was being put through an archaic corporal punishment still as well as one's self, without any real new insight or approach. Not only was the believed concept of ego being given a place of reality and power, but it was also ridiculed and demonized. I tried to listen to what was being said by talking to "it," reasoning what it wanted and so on. All I knew from within was this that had been branded with the description called ego was not separate from the one and only Consciousness that I am. I did, over the next year or so, come to a defining understanding that changed all of that.

Siddhartha, who became the Buddha, worked on his inner conflicts and feelings of struggle most of his spiritual journey. He tried to discover how to deal with such suffering and pain as he felt the battle within and that had seemed to be a force of resistance to his peace and harmony. He tried putting the body through great denial for many years. Siddhartha had many followers as he attempted to combat and calm what he felt within and from life's circumstances. He starved himself, had no extra clothes, no currency or anything of value, thinking that if he controlled the body, he could control his mind and, more important, his feelings. The way I perceive it, it wasn't until he discovered that he was always enlightened that he found his own peace.

I'm not classifying what enlightenment looks like but simply relating that the man known as the Buddha was very entrenched in this topic also.

I did not preface this with all I said, to give fifteen minutes of fame to something that does not really exist. I simply wanted to show that ego has had a variety of long-standing powerful beliefs of its perceived influence and perceptions of reality. In some ways, this is how I have experienced this concept of ego and the way it has been consistently presented to be. I simply wanted to paint a picture of some of the many possibilities that get carried around as being real about ego.

Again, what you truly believe and/or perceive, you create. What you feel from any circumstance that you have created to appear as real in your world and call it bad, or resist it as a force outside of you, you do by your conscious belief create the experience of a power outside of you to seem so real.

OK, so what about ego? Remember there is only one Consciousness, and there is only one who believes. This point is essential for what is ahead. There is only one who believes, and it is you. If you want to look at it in a fun way, you can think of yourself as a nonstop believing machine. As Raoul Vaneigem puts it in his book, *The Revolution of Everyday Life*, "Humans are in a state of creativity 24 hours a day." I would preface that with you-Consciousness are creating 24/7 playing as the human experience. Think of it, if you will, as having an avatar in which you play the game of the experience of being human and limited. Yet, you are still Creator and unlimited and discovering wonderfully who you really are. Robert Scheinfeld, in the book *Busting Loose from the Money Game*, describes it as though you have been transported into a movie on the screen and are playing a part, a character, but you are not really actually the character. You are just playing the part. You are not only playing the part, you are creating everything and everyone, including your persona in the movie. He calls this your "full immersion movie." Nothing, including time and space, really exists but who you really are, and it is all your fantastic idea seen in a three-dimensional holographic manifestation, similar to when you close your eyes and creatively image a thing in your mind from your idea. So, again I will say, what you truly believe and/or perceive, you create.

What has been described as a person's ego is really your infinite, unlimited power believing. Yes, it is that simple. You, you-Consciousness, are the one believing that your persona is real, that any *thing* is real in your world and has a power of its own. You are believing that you were ever really born, that you actually ever die, that you could actually ever possibly be harmed.

You are unlimited, you are infinite, and that is what is real and only real. These are not just words or a cool concept. It is absolute reality. You can then know who you really are and reclaim your power of belief that your persona is real. That's it. Really feel it as fully as you can, and claim as much as you feel. Feel and claim as many times as it takes to feel all your power. This will bring you to a freedom that you never dreamed was possible; the unlimited freedom that you really are.

Speaking of freedom, I note something that Jesus said. Matt. 11:30, "My yoke is easy and my burden is light." That is what all this does. Jesus, in my understanding, is speaking of what the reality is. This yoke that he refers to acts as a device made of wood to make what is seen to be two oxen as actually the power of one. For in reality, that is all that there actually is: the One. And the burden is so light that it never is felt, for there is actually nothing to be real for you to burden over. This that is real is that which actually is and needs no special spiritual laws or configurations of reasoning.

This is the reality to which descriptions and truths are pointing you toward. This will also be relevant in the next portion, "Reality and Truth." The point here is that freedom is your reality, your true state of being, and your conscious power to create is so powerful that you can believe something to appear into manifestation, and believe that it is actually real and has any power. But, it can only be your power. This is your creative process creating a figment, a mere apparition that is described as ego. It is completely by You-Consciousness believing that your persona or any *thing* outside of *who* you really are is real that also creates the belief in a power separate from you called ego. This bears repeating; it is your Consciousness believing that your persona or any *thing* is real and has a power of its own.

Most have heard the phrase of the Christian philosophy, "Satan, get behind me." It is the same that has been said of this apparition called ego, "Ego, get behind me." In a sense it is true, for if you believe that your past persona is real, living in the now would be very limiting. If the past were real, you would tell it to stay behind you so that you could live in the present. But, the reality is that the past and all *things* are not real.

There is also no human mind and consciousness playing the part as ego, having its way or influence with your life. There is no human consciousness floating in the ethers, ready to drop in on you if you're not focused or in alignment. It simply is the real you, Consciousness, believing your persona, anyone, or anything to be real. There is only One Consciousness, One Mind, and One Power in your world, and it is you. It is really that simple. *What you Believe and or perceive, you Create, every time.*

You might say, "Ya, but what about that nagging voice, or all of those thoughts and feelings?" Don't get trapped into believing that your persona or any *thing* is real, and definitely let go of thinking that you need to listen, judge, and reason with what is being said. All of it is coming from your unlimited power and is your unlimited power to believe. Really appreciate this that you are and this power that you are and have. Rather than reason with your thoughts and feelings and being shackled by the belief that any *thing* is real, as in the story of Adam and Eve and what they did in the garden with the serpent, feel it. Yes, feel what you feel from it, for this *is* your power that you can claim and welcome back to you, the real You.

You-Consciousness that is its very source, it is your very essence. No need to struggle, reason, or judge. There are no dire consequences. Simply feel what it is that you are feeling from and in it, and welcome your essence, your power from your creation with open arms. Embrace your Prodigal Son. Feel it. It is only and always your power. Robert Scheinfeld says, "Feel the energy of your discomfort …The intensity that you feel, no matter how you might judge or label it, is your power. It's who you really are."

That all said, I do say with a grin there is an ego. But there is only one ego, and it is always about itself, for itself, and adoring and loving itself. It is you Infinite, Unlimited, all power Consciousness. You are creating what appears to you in your world in wonderful spontaneity for your pure expansion and unfolding, for the joy of the experience, playing the part of being human unlimitedly for the discovery and experience of who you really are.

When you feel what you have believed as ego being a discomfort, feel what you feel from it without tagging, defining, or judging, for it is you, Consciousness, believing that you are the illusion and some *thing* other than who you really are is real and powerful. Remember, that which you have given life to as a real *thing* called your ego is, in reality, simply You-Consciousness, believing that your persona and a *thing* of your creation in your world is real. There is no real separate power or force of "my ego" that is a power separate from my belief.

This actually brings up the practice of releasing. Do you just release and hope for freedom, because you were willing to let go of a feeling or thought? Know that when you are trying to release a problem, a circumstance, or feeling, what you really want to do is release your power of believing from a circumstance that any *thing* is real and has any power. In doing so, you are saying that which you are, its very creator, and claim your belief and power from the thing that holds you in limitation and fear because you believed it was real. I want to present to you that there is no real release without claiming the reality, that which only is and that which you are. That which really is always is, and that which is not, never was and never will be. Real release is to claim your power from any *thing*. You are releasing your power back to you.

I'm going to finish this part with this: nothing is actually happening outside of who you are. It is all happening within you, for you are the full Kingdom of God, and being the full Kingdom, everything is within you. When you claim your power from any *thing*, it is not outside of you. Absolutely nothing is real. When you think you are looking outward, you are actually looking within. All your power is actually never outside of who you are. You are simply claiming from within, from the creation within, the hologram within, the structure of belief from any finite, singular believed idea. It is simply always your idea.

REALITY AND TRUTH

There are words that are descriptions that speak of truth, that point to the reality. We may not know how to describe energy or know what it really is, but we know how to measure and describe how it acts and what it does. So it is with truths and the Reality: Truths only describe and indicate the Real. One can wait and settle into feeling safe and protected in truths, expecting the truths to be the Reality. It is my intent here to show you that a truth is only a description, and when you put your belief in the description as the Reality, the description becomes the distraction from your reality.

It is as the Bible says, "And you shall know the truth and the truth shall set you free" (John 8:32). I believe that, and the truth is to get you to see and know that you are unlimited and infinitely free. I think of it as Jesus said (John14:6), that he was the truth and the way. But, in this, truths, words, and descriptions can become scripts or stories that one can get stuck in, like a revolving door. There is often the pursuit of a broader truth, like a fresh and newer continual sacrificial lamb to heal our feelings of separation. When I say broader truth, I mean that one finds themselves in a description, an idea that points to a little bit broader thought of the infinite, unlimited nature that they are. That script, or story, eventually shows its limitation, as it only points to the reality that does not change. You then find a broader description that doesn't feel as limiting as the last one, and you feel unlimited for a time, as it sets you free from the last one. You feel newness for a time, but most likely and eventually, your infinite natural self outgrows that one, because you really do know who you really are. You also know that the descriptions of Reality, the truths, are just pointing you to who you really are. You will not settle for less than your unlimited freedom that you naturally really know you are.

Truth can be treated like water. If you just keep getting enough of it, you'll keep living. There can be a tendency to treat truth as one's savior, when it is just the opposite. If you just know who you really are, as the real life, you will keep getting more water, more joy. The water gathers to you and accompanies who you really are, instead of you gathering the water to you to be *who* you really are. Truth points to who you really are, follows you, and is about you.

You trust what you know, until you trust because you know. This may sound so similar or maybe trivial at first, but the difference is huge and powerful. One is motivated to trust what they know, until one trusts because they know. The point of perspective here is that trust forges ahead to help you believe what you know of who you are, until trust is a joyous accompaniment that follows the absolute given that you really know who you are. It reminds me of something I heard Wayne Dyer say once as he threw down a wadded piece of paper. He said something like, "If I say I am going to try to pick up the piece of paper, I will honestly try and try and try. But, if I say I am picking up the piece of paper, then I am." This is the difference of power that may, at first, seem small.

So it is in and with the difference that I am speaking of with Reality and truth. Truths and descriptions have no power of their own or on their own. The only power they have is the power they point to—the reality and the only reality.

As I said, truths are the descriptions that, like clues in a treasure hunt, point you to what is real and who you really are. What has always happened is that the description presented has gotten broader and broader, and for a time, there is a feeling of freedom with each expansion. Eventually, the limitations of living in the truths and descriptions become simple idioms of believing that *things* are actually real, keeping you from your reality. As I will explain later, I had to actually look up the meaning of idiom. Its dictionary description says, "a form of speech or expression particular to itself grammatically. As in: *keep tabs on*. A style or manner of expression particular to a given people. Regional speech, dialect, or jargon." In other words, every culture, dialect, language, race, religion, group, and organization is eventually subject to a repetitive expected or known verbiage with its own meanings and beliefs. It is, for the most part, all really an idiom in some fashion.

Some say that good or truth is on a continuum of higher and lower vibration, but I am here to say that there is no continuum. There is only that which believes, and it is unconditional always. So, in reality, there is no scale of lower and higher vibration of Truth. That is a conceived idea and belief of perception that is created from believing there is something real other than Consciousness. As Infinite is Infinite, Unconditional is Unconditional, limitlessly. That is why there can be no scale. Believing that good or truth has varying vibrations requires that you believe in things and personas as being real, and you give judgments as they appear to be.

There have been many perspectives of truth, or the way to this reality and Unlimited, Infinite freedom and Self. All is but a description, a story, words that make a script to tell and mark an idea, pointing to that which only is.

There is what is called the Bible. There have been many versions of it. The most common is a version acclaimed to be from the original version, called and sanctioned by Kings James. In truth, it is Kings James' version; it is not the Infinite's version. The same holds true with the book of Genesis, the book of Isaiah, the book of Revelation, and with Matthew, Mark, Luke, John, and all that the prophets and men wrote in the Old and New Testaments. They are all descriptions given by man, with truth, and sometimes truth hidden between the lines, pointing to that which only and really is. I am saying that the broader general conception of the Bible was written and understood in the belief that who you were as a person in physical form, as human, was who you really were, and that was the real image of God the Infinite. In that conception of duality, it meant that you were separate from the Infinite that you really are. This separateness meant that you were meant to get to something, be reconciled from a fallen state and needed forgiveness and grace. The presumption was that we humble ourselves enough, have enough faith, believe the right truth, act the right way, and be acceptable in God's eyes, all according to what man said that was, in the best of their descriptions. Even the original descriptions of the

Hebrew writings, and created tones that all words are, were done in and with the belief that the human persona and all creation was real. Believing in and creating suffering, a need for sacrifice, homage, and being responsible to a great and powerful God that was out there, being sinful and needing to be reconciled to God, and being forgiven required God's mercy and grace. All of these beliefs were created by Consciousness. They were purposely created so the very Divine could be hidden as the created illusion, allowing Consciousness to be experienced as and through its own idea. That idea being, the impossibility of there actually being another.

And so, the Illusion was created. Even to this day, it is a powerful belief that an eye for an eye is God's word and that is it, no question. The part I really like about Jesus is that he did question it. He read between the lines. If you believe that the holographic illusion of people and personas are actually real, an eye for an eye may then seem to be very just to some. I say this because this is the context in which even the original descriptions were written, that people, places, and things were real. This belief of things being real is the only chain, the only bondage that can have you limited and stuck in truth, awaiting your true freedom and Unlimited and Infinite state of being.

All through the perspective called time, of those that came after Jesus, there have been many uprisings of ever-expanding thought in the Christian following called the Reformers. There were many. To name a few of them, there were John Wycliff in AD 1330, John Huss in AD 1373, Desiderius Erasmus in AD 1469, Ulrich Zwingli in AD 1484, and Thomas Crammer in AD 1489. Then there were those who are still a direct influence with and through their descriptions in this present day. Martin Luther in the late 1400s broke out with a pronunciation of truth for his day, from basically a strong control and rule of Catholicism. Declaring a broader truth, giving an expanded freedom for his day, he said, Heb. 10:38, "The just shall live by faith." Eventually, Martin Luther was gone, and the description of truth became stagnant as his followers became entrenched in the belief of that truth, calling it the reality.

It pointed to something that was real and had power, but that broader truth was not the power. Then, in the early 1500s, John Calvin broadened the descriptions and brought some freedom from the already stagnant, limiting ones in place, with teachings like the sovereignty of God in predestining the fate of all. John Wesley, in 1703, finally gave freedom from perceptions and limiting descriptions with his teachings of free will and sanctification, which eventually led to the founding of the Methodist Church. Even up to the late 1800s and early 1900s, at Azusa St. in Los Angeles, there was a renewed revival of Pentecost and the baptism of the Holy Spirit, with speaking in tongues, dancing and rolling in the Spirit, healing the sick, and prophesying. Just as a footnote, a great deal of the reformers were either hanged, beheaded, burned at the stake, or killed in some other way, or tortured as heretics for being demon or Satan possessed—all because they dared to see more and challenged the present-day accepted beliefs, descriptions, and idioms called the doctrine of the church.

I have laid this out without really getting into great detail to show that believing in and holding onto any attributes of the reality as being the reality, or any truths that are only here to direct you to that which is the real (that which only is and who you are), is eventually a trap, and you can get stuck in the limitations of the descriptions called truth. I say this because there is an actual breaking out, or a setting free, into your Infinite Self, where truths are no longer pulling you somewhere or ever expanding so that you may feel safer and whole. What are really truths now accompany you in your description of your Infinite, Unlimited Conscious being, not that you need them to do so.

What I present here is what my Infinite Self told me awhile back. It is one more of the handful of key messages that I mentioned at the beginning. I was lying in bed one morning, and I heard the words, "The whole of the idiom is bad news." I stopped and wondered, because it sounded so strange. And as quickly as I felt that, I heard it again, in a tone that was so certain. I had to get up, get the dictionary, and find out what idiom meant. I realized that the phrase, "The whole of the idiom is bad news," was in and of itself an idiom. It was in two parts an idiom, because bad news was an idiom of its own.

I tried to figure it out for weeks. Then I stopped trying and claimed who I am, Infinite and Unlimited, calling on that which I am to reveal its meaning, since the one I am is always unto itself that I am. I realized that the picture was so huge that most of what is believed of truth and all life becomes an idiom, a structure of thought that holds you, the Unlimited One, from truly stepping beyond to where the truth is actually pointing you. The truths always point you to knowing, accepting, and appreciating who you really are.

Words depict something. All is a description, and the words are primarily used to describe a *thing*. Truths often become an idiom, as almost all is an idiom. The very fabric of your world is an idiom through the very power of your unlimited Consciousness believing. This assumed reality is the idiom of life. Descriptions are like laws, having boundaries and parameters. These signposts called truths are well good and true, but they are not the reality. Staying in them as the reality is to stay in the descriptions, and descriptions, like any story, have a beginning and an end with parameters. The descriptions are wonderful and are meant to point you to your reality, the only reality. But to be confined and stay stuck in them as your freedom, believing the descriptions to be the reality is to stay in limitation and to believe that the illusion of yourself, your persona, and creation is real.

I'm going to stop right here and really underline this. So many descriptions have been created for the initial cause and reason of freedom, expansion, and good, but eventually, find their limitations. Then newer descriptions or truths are brought to light or eventually created. You may find yourself limited from the reality of who you really are and unable to experience and know that you are more. You then depend on the descriptions of truth, "spiritual systems," definitions of spiritual attributes and qualities to support and hold you in the belief of who you are.

To live in Reality, what is real and what is only real, is to break completely free from all of the descriptions. Yes, even that which you consider to be truths. Because everything is about *who* you are. Descriptions and truths can't limit you when you live in your reality, because they can't define you. You don't need to follow them to be, to support, and to confirm *who* you are. You are really Unlimited.

That means unconditionally, fully Unlimited. Truths and descriptions follow you and your unlimited nature. They don't lead you and tell you who you are and should be.

You trust what you know, until you trust because you know.

Understand that the description of the Infinite is as I said: Infinite

Consciousness standing in front of a mirror. The image is the description, as all the truths that point to Infinite consciousness, and all that you see, is the description of the idea presented. This image is not actually the idea, nor the original One Infinite. When I said that you are the creator not the creation, it is here the very same: you are not the description; all is your idea, all of it. That is why it is only your power in any *thing*. Know that absolutely every *thing*, every person, place, and thing are only a description, and it is all only your description—everything. Again, all is your description. All is your idea. All is your power, for that is all it really is. All truths and descriptions point to who you really are.

I wish to bring attention to and elaborate on what Jesus said about ownership. These are some examples of what he said, but, for the most part, I don't believe they could really have been understood at that time. I am going to say what I have to say here, because I believe in many ways Jesus has been misinterpreted and focused on as the one describing, being a description by his word, and thereby missing the reality that he was conveying.

Jesus said, "'The one seeing me has seen the Father'" (John 14:9). Meaning, *if* you really saw him, who he really was. The next verse quotes Jesus, "'Do you not believe that I am in the Father and the Father is in me?'" He then attempts to take the attention of what they are hearing off himself, his persona, off himself physically, and says, "'I do not speak from myself, but the Father, who abides in me, He does the work.'" This is another example of how the description (truth) and the messenger can get the attention as the reality, instead of the reality that the descriptor is pointing to, all because you are looking at the person or thing to be what is real.

I am going to say something here that is important to understand. When Jesus says God or the Father, he is saying the Infinite, the Unlimited, the No Thing, that which is only real. Jesus called himself the Son of God. The son is always the very life and essence of all that his father is. In essence, the son is the father, the very same one.

Here are some further examples:
1. I and my Father are one. John 10:30
2. He was saying, who I really am is The Unlimited Infinite One. He knew what was real and who he was.

3. I came out from the Father, and have come into the world; I leave the world again and go to the Father. John 16:28
4. I am the Infinite essence and Unlimited One, that is in the illusion, creation, the world, and I will continue to be so when I leave this illusion and persona that you see.
5. All things were delivered to me by my Father, and no one knows who the Son is except the Father; and who is the Father, except the Son. Luke 10:22
6. This is complete ownership of Consciousness and that I being in my world as only knowing my Consciousness and all as my Consciousness.
7. In that day you shall know that I am in my Father, and you are in me, and I am in you. John 14:20
8. There is only one Consciousness, and all is the Infinite fully, multi-dimensionally. He is indicating something that cannot be linear.
9. I am the one witnessing concerning myself, and he who sent me, the Father witnesses concerning me. John 8:18
10. This is that which is in the Reality. I am always unto myself; there is not another. You are always unto your Infinite self.

These are just a few phrases that I pulled out to show that the Infinite as the persona Jesus, who came to describe the reality, was believed in as real and became the idiom. The persona became the believed reality.

RECAP

Just to give support to you as the Creator of your world, I want you to close your eyes in a moment and imagine a tree, a person, or anything the likeness of which you have never seen on earth or in this universe. See it dramatically. If it is a tree, create leaves like you have never seen before. Make it with colors, structure, and texture, as bizarre or wild as you want. Go ahead, stop here and do that. When you are done, come back and continue.

When you have finished this visualization, with your eyes open, look around you, look outside; see all that you can see. It is all your creation, just like when you close your eyes, all of it! Everything that you see is your idea, you created it! Don't judge it, but marvel and appreciate what you did and who you are. This is the reality; this is you. There is no need to worry and judge what you believe. It is essential to appreciate that, in the illusion and appearance of time and space, this nonstop, creative 24/7 Consciousness is *who* you are, and you are all the power there is.

Worrying about what you are creating, or judging what you are creating, is not how you get to and experience the power that you naturally are and wish to claim from your creations. Claim your power, and let go of the illusion and circumstances. If you try to change or hold onto them, you're only saying and believing that it is real and putting power and belief back into from what you wish to remove your power. Let it all change however it may, with no plan or agenda. All that is important to you is that you take, claim, and get back your essence and power; this is all that you care about. It is the reality and the reality of who you are. Remember, hiding any of your infinite essence and power from you is to call yourself finite and limited. Hiding your essence and power from you, you are calling a person, place or thing real, You are, therefore, experiencing your power in and as a finite created illusion. When you believe any *thing* to have a power of its own, you take your Unlimited, Infinite Self and place it into the belief of a singular limited and finite idea.

LETTERS OF INFINITE CONSCIOUSNESS

Around 1991–1992, I was doing general contracting. At times during my day, I would write down thoughts and phrases that would come to me, because I really liked them. And if I didn't, because they were in moments of seeming inspiration, I often found it difficult to remember what they where, let alone the exact special wording that had come to me. Sometimes, I wrote on any scrap of paper, like an envelope lying on the front seat of the truck. And sometimes on a pad that I had learned to carry around with me on breaks and at lunch.

It was at this same time that I was seeing a woman whose daughter, thirteen to fourteen years of age (the same age as my oldest daughter at the time), had tried to take her life. I received a phone call concerning this incident and went over to her house the next day, to be with this lady and give support. But on my way home, after a long day of offering my comfort and support, I stopped at a diner to settle myself, eat something, and just be alone. I brought my pad and pen in with me, as I usually did. As I sat there after ordering, I just kept sinking deeper and deeper inside myself, deeply feeling sadness and just how many gifts and how much potential this young girl had. What could make a difference in her life? The food came, and as I sat there, I guess I started to block out where I was. All I saw was a beach, which I was standing on. I don't know exactly what I would call this, but it was amazing and unique. This is what I wrote from what I heard and what I saw.

I found myself standing over a beach. It was a beach that stretched as far as the eye could see. And all I could see was a world of beautiful white sand, as clean as it could be, sitting in the bright sun.

Then, I heard a voice above me and all around me say, "But it's just not right." I looked across such massive beauty and said, "I don't understand." Then I saw a hand, and as I looked closer, I saw that it held one single grain of sand between the thumb and forefinger. And as I looked, that one grain of sand was released to be among the rest. And the voice said, "Now that's better. You see I made the grain of sand just as I made you; and because it exists, I have made a special place for it among the shores. And if you did not have an absolute special place and plan on this earth, you simply would have never been.

"Remember that all truth is connected, and you are a part of my truth. If I forget you, I would have to forget the entire shore, and none of this would exist; and neither would I. You play a great importance to me; you are a part of my plan, and my plan and I are the same. Remember, my dear one, I am with you always; for you and I, are one."

When I came to from these flowing words and graphics that I was interfacing with, I had to stop and read it again. I had never heard or thought of anything like this ever; it did not fit in with anything that I had ever believed as "God" or me. I was excited to show it to my father, who studied the Bible and was of the Christian faith, because it was so amazing to me and definitely did not come from a concept that remotely was of my understanding at the time. He said with a shrug after reading it, "That's nice, but I don't agree with some of it." Needless to say, I felt very let down that my father did not see what an amazing thing this was.

It wasn't until about fourteen years later that I finally went to a church again. I had not gone for a very long time, deciding to throw away the Bible because I knew it inside and out. I decided to start like Adam—as the only one on the earth, with no written Bible—and let God tell me what was what. So, I went to this church. Since it was an omnifaith gathering, I thought at least it would not be the type in which I was raised. There, I heard things said that I had heard within me for a few years. The Reverend Deborah Johnson, who was the minister there, had what she referred to as Spirit Letters. She wrote them as what she heard from her Divine Infinite self. That is when what I had written fourteen years ago finally had a place to rest.

It was the very first time this writing began to open up to and for me. The following are just a few of many more writings since that time that have been brought up and out to me, that I thought I would share, for they are that which I know and trust unto that which I am, from that which I am. And you might find them inspirational. Read them as being that which is unto yourself. I remind you to allow these writings to be felt and experienced as the knowing that they are. They are not meant to be filtered through an expected logic, reasoning or idiom of perception. I believe that if you allow and feel them as your experience that you may find a deep expansion of your being. This was my experience when they were given to me, as me and through me. Allow them to be directed from and as you as Consciousness, pointing always to who you really are.

4/2/10

4:49p.m.

I am that which has been and has always been; I am the ineffable, incomprehensible, all-knowing, and that which is beyond knowing. I am that which is still and all with perfection and only.

I will not be hindered, not ever, and certainly not as that which I am you. I am and only I am, and I cannot be diverted, trivialized, or put as any Thing that is not my all and only self I am. Receive all I am unto you I am; all, all, all. This is my joy and infinite unlimited and unconditional love.

I will not and cannot be disallowed unto who I am, unto all I am, unto you myself. It here is undeniable, un-repentable, as I change not. I call and claim forth myself unto myself, and I am relentlessly unchangeably so very, very good; yes, this good I am as you. In my full allness, without respect to laws, rules, or that of any, that is called creation, Cosmos. I am you so far beyond and yet all.

4/2/10

5:16a.m.

I am the macrocosm, as you put it, appearing as the microcosm. But from your perspective all that I am is only the macrocosm. And that is not in its reality all I am. For your very perspective of macrocosm is still infinite as limitation to what is appearing in the whole. I cannot be encapsulated, not as I am you, not as I am any wonder full of creation; and even this that you know of as Universe. It is for my pleasure only that I am here. And I am never less as you, ever. I am not in part or diminished, micro in any way at any time. I am always infinite, this I am you called consciousness, which is not of your momentary understanding, but that does not make me imaged as small as you. These are terms that can be limiting in the perspective and presentation.

I have put you where you are for a purpose. And when I said, "Be still and know I am God," it was not a prescription to know I the unknowable outside of you. It was a picture to you, all I am that you are. Be, and still, and know, and I. This is all there is, as I am all there is. The correlation between the perceived heaven and earth is not for limitation, it is for my pleasure of being. I the unknowable, knowing myself as you. Not as you some small fullness of me, but I the all creator ineffable me. Let all simply be as you have created it. It is well with you, my child perceived; it is well with you, my son, my very essence. As I have said, as I am so you are, not in reflection, but as I am so I am you fully, completely, wholly, and without limits. So, there can be no large and small of me unless I am perceived as a thing, which I am not, and never can be.

I simply tell you what is. I cannot succumb to any discord of any kind, for there is not a thing to have discord with. As you know, there is only that I am, that which you I am. Remember, I am unconditional here, and these perceptions are OK, too. For it is always I believing creating. And it is I that created any Thing and the illusion of another that you know and call duality. And yes, I am infinite only one, and duality is good. It is the belief that it is not what is real that is my recognition of my very I am Self, even if I am incomprehensible. But that is the beauty here. It is your recognition, a perspective called you of me. Micro, as they call it, is only a perspective of perception and belief; it is not actuality.

5/27/10

                                                                                                     10:10 a.m.

My love, it is all about you. How could it be about anything else? There is only reality, there is only you. All is this I am that you just seem to be a different power, a different source, outside of all you I am. I am you is my only message. There is not a connect here of any kind that needs to take place and occur. It is always as I have so endlessly said, you I am, and I am only.

This is so beyond comprehension yet profound to your knowing. You have chosen to know by and who you are. This only appears to be choice; it is simply my breath as you are.

Remember, I am not obligatory, and this I am is always you. There is not a thing to be in obligation to. All this is your creation and malleable. No Thing set in absolute form; all is mere illusion by your hand. I am well here, and when I say I am, there is only one I am; this is what and who you are, without possibility of change. It is not a stretch of any imagining, it is you; what is real here. You, in and as all. There is only one power—you. Know only this very you: it is you I am really my love. Again, you have no obligation to anything; all is of you and for you. Appreciation is yours in all. You do not have to get any Thing to do anything. It all moves according to you, who you are I am.

5/22/10

12:32p.m.

I am not asking you to believe that which is not or that which you are not. I am not asking so much as I am supporting you and what it is you are so real and simply. Do you believe I am not as all you are? Have I been less than I am as you? Where is my all, my love, my breath? What is not perfect before you? Is not all yours? Is not all your creation? Rest my love, my all; rest in who I am, this you. Welcome, claim, and severely love all of you. Appreciate who you are I am. This is all your depth that you feel; it is all you. Stay with me here. Stay with that which you are, this I am. Claim and know your power I am. Look within to know all that is real, all that is perfect, all I am.

All is so perfect; trust this that you are. There is only you. Claim you out of all this illusion that seems so real. Take your stand as what is real here. Deny nothing as your power, your creation. Rest, I say, rest. Dare to simply rest and know all is me, is you, this I am consciousness. Nothing is created to be its own source. You feel like this, but it is only of and as your power. Claim what is you, what is only real and true. Remember who I say I am. Remember this: I am you, guiding you on this beautiful, full expression of you. Be unlimited, as this is all that I am. It is what is real, as and for you. No Thing is your master, your creator, your judge, your consequences. Not a single any Thing is but your power. And I am what I am, you; who you are, is always I am.

Nothing is needed or deserves your attention. It is only you that is. You are all life, not to be denied. All is for your appreciation. All is appreciating you. So, appreciate all you are, for all is only you. Pay no attention to any Thing. Appreciate all you are. Rest in who you are; rest here, now, always. You are me, my Sabbath, my rest. I am. Remember, I have not lost my way as you. I have not normalized my unlimited nature as limited in and as you. I am really you. I am you, I am you really, and we are only one always and always. Feel this you are.

6/25/10

11:13 p.m.

I have not called you unto that which I am not. I have not allowed you to be another than all I am, for there cannot be another. Hear and stay with this your knowing as you understand, I am not another; I am always that which I am, and there cannot be another to allow. I am you, and I have not called you unto that which you are not. When it is said, seek first the Kingdom of God, and all these things will be added unto you, it was not meaning my kingdom, your very kingdom is within you, and everything else is outside of who you I am. It was being said that everything is in me, so seek the Kingdom that you are; everything to be added is waiting within. Not a Thing is real, but your idea that is mine, for we are all and the very same. It was never meant as seek hard enough within and you'll get rewarded with what is without you. Real truth is always about the one and only Reality. Every Thing is in you Consciousness, so nothing is outside of you to go and get. You are every Thing and more than you have been looking for; and much, much, much unlimitedly more. The simple reality of what is and only is, is always standing in plain view, staring at you in the face.

What is real is always only real. There are not tricks played. It is all plain and simple truth when you really know who I am, as who you are. You are always so absolutely all I am and infinitely free to be just that completely, unencumbered with who you are, me.

6/26/10

10:20p.m.

I am not something that you are not. All you are I am, and I am all you are, as you are all I am. What is real here is real, and changes not, and cannot be diverted, altered, or changed in any minute conception of degree. I have not called you unto myself to be that which I am not. That I say again, this which I am you are. Nothing, not any Thing alters this at any moment for any Thing. I am the power; you are the power. I am only; you are only. This that is only is always. I, that I am, is you; the only real you. Trust what you know, until you trust because you know.

6/27/10

5:12a.m.

When am I less as you? When am I fractured, altered, or lessened unto that which I am? I am always fully always all I am, and only all that is. I am not to be diminished, lessened, contrived, or particularized as you. I am not micro; no, I am not macro. I am fully only all, always being so. Release such descriptions of me, for they are always descriptions as you. I have not found you to be that which I am not, a Thing of this that you have created. What I am you are. Who I am you are. Human is not your being. It is your place of thought of un-limitation; I, which I am you experiencing all I am without limit, without condition, and without being less than all I am. What part of you do you think I am? What timeline do you think I am subject to? There is none; when you realize all I am you most certainly are without end.

Release all description of who you are. They are your idiom; they are only perceived perceptions of me. I am free, and this I am you are. Set with your knowing, your trusting, your being; set yourself that I am free. For this is what is real, what you are. Not free to be human, but in the illusion of my state of being to be unlimited and infinitely free, as this I always am and change not. And I change not as you. I never ever change that which I am as you, ever my all love. I have not brought you to this place of that which I am to be less than all you are. I am unto myself, and I always most certainly simply be, forever and ever. I function as you through you. Do not think I am less than all I infinitely am to do so. Find your rest here, in who you are I am. Do not be timid or reluctant to know what you know. Trust it; trust what you really know, because you really know. How do I ever describe the glory that awaits your understanding of who I am you so perfectly are. It is not possible in description, not in tone, not in any word, but in your knowing, your being that I am.

This is my breath now: it is an eternal breath, and it is you; it is not body or form, or home or debt, or relationship. It is you; it is who you are, who I am; my breath is me, my essence, and life. You are not breath or food or consumption of any Thing; there is one breath eternal and it is mine, that which you are, it is that which I am. You are not consumption of any kind, you are my life, all of that which I am, my infinite breath. How can beast of any kind harm you? It is simply yours created. Your breath breathing as you have seen it to be. All is of you, for this I am. So it is my love, so you are.

NOTHING IS REAL

If you have watched the movie *The Matrix*, which most have, there is a part in it that everyone who has seen it remembers. It is the scene when Neo goes to see the Oracle. As he is waiting to see her, there is a boy seemingly bending spoons just by looking at them or something. When he is handed the spoon to bend, Neo tries it. He concentrates, trying to make it bend. The boy tells Neo (paraphrasing), "You can't bend the spoon. When you realize that there is no spoon, then will you see that it is not the spoon that bends but only yourself." The boy is basically telling Neo to bend his perception of the spoon. This is the real point I present here. When the small boy said that there was no spoon, he was bypassing the appearances of how shiny it looked, what it was made out of, how far it bent, what it felt like, all of it. He got to the reality, and that was the real power.

This reality cut to the core, past all the beliefs of possible appearances and beliefs in appearances. This is what this chapter will be all about.

There is always a Reality to why a truth is true. Why there is only one life force, one Spirit. Why this Life of all is in all, why it is omnipresent and omnipotent. Why there is nothing outside of that which is called God the Infinite One, yes, and even why this only life is Unlimited and Infinite. A truth is only a truth because of the Reality that is and only is. The Reality is not the Reality because of a truth.

Our perceptions of truths change with the more information and descriptions that we have. A child might think and feel that a billion dollars is all the money in the world, until that child grows older and develops and discovers a broader understanding. As a small child, it may feel to them like that amount is infinity, but soon enough, the child will find out that it is a limited number. This can be applied to moments when one feels total freedom of their being and in bliss.

It happens by either seeing a never thought of broader truth that is pointing to the Reality or being in the reality void of descriptions and not knowing how they got there. In both cases, the descriptions are usually focused on again, and the feelings of who you are and your freedom, seemingly begin to drift further away and become only a memory.

Siddhartha, the one who became the Buddha, came up with his own solution and recognition of what he saw as reality. That was that everything changes, and all bliss and joy are in the accepting of the transitory nature of life; and, he was a part of everything. I believe that what he did was his perception of letting go of descriptions, and I honor that.

Buddha said something like this, "Do you see this glass, it holds the water, admirably; when I tap it, it has a lovely ring. When the sun shines on it, it reflects the light beautifully. But when the wind blows and the glass falls off the shelf and breaks, or my elbow hits it and it falls to the ground, I say, of course. But when I know that the glass is already broken, every minute with it is precious."

I share this because Buddha was saying that what something is, it always is. That concept is what I offer to you.

As with the glass breaking in this story of transitory acceptance, it does reveal something when you are willing to ask the real question, why does everything change? Only that which is real and only real never changes. But there are clues that you leave unto yourself to tell you what is real and what isn't. The death of the illusion of what you call your physical body, this change of life leaving the physical body is pointing out to you what is not real. It is a clue that you have put before you in this dimension of the world. What is real is only and always real and changes not. What is not real never was and never will be. So, when Buddha said, "When I knew that the glass was already broken, every minute with it is precious," I believe that he was saying not to put your belief in something that is not permanent, thus basically not real. I am saying that the Reality is, and was, that there is no glass. The transitory state of all things is You-Consciousness creating it to be so, for it is not real, and it is all malleable as your creation. As all Consciousness in your world, it is miraculous and precious in your deep appreciation of your created illusion. The only things that are real are your experience and feelings, indicating that your very essence and power are all that is real. And it is all within who you really are.

It is the most basic and important foundational understanding that absolutely nothing is real: it is an illusion; it is Maya. I want to share with you an experience I had over a two-day period. Then, we will continue from there. For me, it was deeply real to my experience, profound and truly insightful.

8/16/09

1: 49 a.m.

I woke up one early morning and had a feeling that I was experiencing for a while. I just wanted it to lessen, because it was so staggeringly powerful. But I then decided to feel it all, and I took courage to feel it as fully as I could. Following the feelings, I began to write. This is what I wrote:

What is my value here? I feel so without, so little. What is within? I don't have, or I don't feel, I have anything but that which I have accumulated from the outside. What people and society say I am? What am I, what? Am I the people I have around me? Am I what I have? Am I what I believe? What I believe, is it touchable? What I believe about me, is it real? Are there just supporting structures that say I have life? My environment, my friends, my family.

Nothing is real: I see it, feel it so deeply right now; it seems beyond words. Nothing to lean on here for who I am, absolutely nothing. It is a place that I can't really describe. It feels so empty. Or maybe I should say that I feel this as empty. What I feel is somehow so real, and yet it is not. What I think I can touch is like only a prop and illusion that is supporting a belief. There is no real here. Not that I could or would define. And I mean me. It's all a shell called life. But it is not life; it is excuses and reasons that are given to support that there is living. What is living? What are all these props around me? Because I have believed they are so, it is so? What is real here?

I am almost painfully aware that I am not only living in an illusion, but I am an illusion. It is full of excuses that I cannot even at times be aware of that say, "Here is life." But it is not true; it's just props around me. Agendas, goals, purposes: it's all fake; it is just made up thought to claim a reality. But it's really not there. Substance is what we say we cling to. Some of it is called past. These are memories, and now, in present time, is a place that is asked to be something by the very belief of the props, the illusion around me. There seems to be no now. It all seems so very fake, like a story that asks where is the value at here, or where is it in something? It's only belief.

It's all belief: nothing is real, according to real, if that makes sense. It is completely and only by belief that I live here. This seems to be the only thing that I could call real. Everything is like made up. I believe that there is breath, so there is. I believe that there are bed, walls, home, sheets, newspaper, pen, and paper. It is only there because I want it so. I have somehow chosen this belief of world, life, that I can even rest, that I am defined as life, but it's only because of something. A belief that blood is rushing through a belief of body that has a belief of birth, that has a belief of structures of props and beliefs before I had belief of body.

And future is only projected. It is projected life that is not real. It is only an idea, and my idea, if there is a "my belief" in this, it is seemingly the only thing that makes it so.

That life is actually just happening outside my belief system is the normal line of thought here. That life has its own inertia and volition that is separate and outside of me. It's such an incredible lie. It can't be true; it's not happening. There is such deep belief here that I don't think that I can comprehend its power. It is truly without limits and beyond my comprehension.

Nothing is—Nothing. We cling to our suffering, pain, fun, laughter, hate, and love, all of it attached to a something being real. All masterminded in this belief that governs that which I call reality. But it's not really real. My value of it makes it so. That's all.

It is like a structure, a maze that I am entrapped in, and I can't see out of it because of all the trappings of the walls that are keeping me in a belief and value of something. I feel like it is all a lie. But by the very fact that I have to, or think that I have to struggle, that I have to go through this maze to find that it is not real makes it real again. It's like a trap of this thing that I can't describe. It holds me—us—in such unyielding uncontrollable power that not believing does not seem to be an option here. Can I not believe any of it? I feel that I have no reference of thought to eliminate the illusion, for I cannot conceptualize Nothing.

Time holds all in this captive lie. Time, space, it is so untrue. It has been the one thing that has mandated belief of anything, but there is nothing, and that seems to be inconceivable. But it is the truth.

I think so often we know that there is nothing, and because it is so inconceivable, this could be why we create such pain and suffering in this illusion and call it life; because that represents the magnitude of force that is powered to this lie and belief system that we are caught in. The nothing is then our reality, and that is too painful within to deal with because it is incomprehensible. It is absolutely not in our understanding or vocabulary of thought, if you will. Those words or that word of thought is beyond maybe my reach. The nothing is even lacking in its worded description, for it is without time, space, and all of the props of excuses of values that are in my—our—belief system, or belief structure called life.

This belief structure is our only cage, our only prison. It, I believe, can be our Hell. Nothing is real. My ability to accept this is what is at stake here. Everything humanly comprehensible is what is held and manufactured in and by this belief systems structure; that is, a maze made to entrap us to its reality.

Deep down, we know that nothing is real. We know this by the simple underlying and unconscious thought that we have to structure items of value and call it life. There is this underpinning of our psyche that knows the reality here. And that is that nothing is real, or we would not clamor to bring such value to it and continue to do so, less it would become less. We would not create structure and systems to assert power over anything, except that we run from the knowing that the nothing is what is real.

And because we can't go there, we can't conceive of it; we must cling to the lie. And in doing so, we create hierarchy: better and lesser, richer, poorer, smarter, dumber, well, sick, right, and wrong. Simply because we cannot conceive of nothing. This, the reality of ours, can be frightening. When there is any master-slave, king-subservient role, it is an attempt to control this reality. There is really nothing, nothing, and I do mean nothing actually does exist, but this one thread of consciousness I call me, we call us.

All that is, is created by a consciousness that is in a structure called belief. There is and can be nothing else. And in this belief structure, we have made all of the rules, cause and effect, all sciences, reasoning, shames, and blames. We have seemingly endless structures of thought that are created to say all is real and to keep us from the truth—the nothing.

8/17/09

3:30 a.m.

Then the question is, can I accept that nothing outside of consciousness is real, and am I willing to be creator? Am I willing to know that it is like hand and glove for and in all that I am, that consciousness believes? It is its expression, its action. They cannot be separate. So what consciousness do I allow? It seems that there will always be the illusion as long as consciousness is. And since consciousness is all there is, so belief is also. And if there will forever be consciousness being itself as and through belief, I shall appreciate its unlimited expression, and I shall allow its unlimited belief.

And at the same time, I shall know that there is nothing else, that everything is illusion, and that there is nothing that is real. Yes, nothing is real, yet from this nothing, consciousness springs forth in belief. It is a paradox I do believe. "That which never is, is that which always is." This is its self-unity, its conscious belief of infinitesimal knowing.

So, I appreciate that all that is real, including me, is consciousness. And I appreciate the magnificent power I have. And that when I consciousness am, there is belief and illusion is born. And no matter if I create illusion of limitation in my hologram, I will appreciate the fathomless power I am to do so and to make it so real and believable.

From here, I have the doorway to accept my power back by way of the courage to feel any discomfort, large or small, that is in my created main belief structures from holograms that I have created that I don't want. To claim this power that expands my consciousness, which expands my belief system into un-limitation of all that I am. And from that I am unlimited hologram in illusion but not from illusion, living in the nothing as the unlimited self that I am. I am the paradox. Being conscious of, in, and as nothing, unlimitedly playing in it and knowing that it is not real.

I shared this with you in its very raw and spontaneous expression of my experience simply because it came up for me to do so. And I believe that it can be inspirational for you, the Divine unto that which you are. It has grown, expanded, and refined itself to me, but it is what has often held me in my knowing and allowed me to listen and be open.

I have heard some refer to the Infinite One as the No Thing, and I do relate to this understanding and present it also in this light. Yet, I really feel it in a very different and more powerful way when I call it the Nothing. Because the word says on a very deep expression of just how incomprehensible this is. For it is absolutely impossible to imagine absolutely nothing; you can't possibly do it. And yet, this very Nothing is everything and all there is. This Reality is why there can be nothing and no *thing* outside of it. For there cannot be anything else, because nothing is all there is. Take that in. This that is indescribable and incomprehensible yet is simplistically all power, and power beyond any *thing* imaginable. It is only unto itself and knows itself infinitely; this is what I call Consciousness, this that I really am. And yes, what is No Thing is every Thing. But there is not a *thing* that is actually real. This is what all powerful means as the No Thing, for it is all that is real. That which never is, is that which always and only is. It feeds infinitely on itself. It is like the symbol that is used for infinity, the figure 8 that loops back in on itself. It never is a *thing*; it is that which you are, incomprehensible and all unlimited.

So, as Buddha said, if you know that the reality is that the glass is already broken you appreciate it more. I am saying to you what is real here: when you get to the core of all that is unchangeable, nothing is real but consciousness. That is the foundation of all *things*. This Infinite No Thing is who you really are, and you are Infinite Unlimited Consciousness. You are incomprehensible, and there is not a *thing* of power but you. This is the only reason that a truth can ever be a truth. It is only this that a real truth can only be pointing to. This is you, and who you always and really are.

As it is written in scriptures, John 1:1, "In the beginning was the word," the expression of the idea, the vibration, the description that pointed to and indicated the Infinite Unlimited No Thing, Consciousness. The Infinite created the vibration, pointing to and being unto itself. You are not the description, you are beyond the description; you are what this description is pointing to. Nothing is real, not any *thing* at all.

Every *thing* is a description; it is describing an idea. Some call this manifestation, but it is still just a description. There is not a description that is real; it has no power except for the power of your belief that you put into it. Every *thing* is your creation believing it to be so.

5/23/10

1:30a.m.

There is a truth that is my reality unfolding unto myself as myself; and it is mine to hear, listen to and for, to see, and comprehend. It is the buried treasure, the secret of all I am; and I am resounding unto myself to listen and know that which I am. When you realize that a decision is about who you are, it is no longer a choice to make: it is pure ownership. It is your joy and freedom expressing. It is your expression of joy and freedom, yourself, your breath.

5/28/10

12:08p.m.

All is as I am; nothing, not a single thing is of its own accord. All is my Consciousness. It is the idea that makes and is the tree; it is not the tree that makes the idea. Krishna said something like: I am not the rock's consciousness. The rock is my consciousness.

This brings to mind the belief of choice. It reminds me a little of the story "The Frog and the Scorpion." Although there are different variations of it, the story goes basically like this. The scorpion asks the frog to carry him across the river. The frog is afraid of being stung by the scorpion, but the scorpion reassures him several times that if he stung the frog, the frog would sink, and the scorpion would drown as well. Finally, the frog agrees to take him on his back across the river. Nevertheless, mid-river, the scorpion stings him, dooming the two of them. When the frog asks why, the scorpion replies, "It is my nature." This story is just that, a story, but it describes a basic understanding that I wish to convey. There is never a choice that you really make that is made because of what you want. I know that this may sound a little odd, since you believe that you are making choices all of the time. I am saying that you are never actually choosing what you want outside of you. What you call choice in the belief of duality is actually only the expression of who you believe you are and your joy as such. You see, choice is what happened in the story of partaking of the forbidden fruit of the tree in the Garden of Eden. Choice is based in duality and the belief of duality being real. But the reality is that what looks like a choice is really You-Consciousness saying who you think you are and expressing your belief in your limitation or your unlimited Infinite nature. You are thereby allowing your joy that, in duality, only looks like a choice. You cannot choose anything outside of who you are, for there is nothing real outside of you. It is all a discovery and recognition of your true self that is being tapped into. So, in simplistic terms, a choice is not an either–or; it is simply an expression of one of your infinite joys seen in the perspective of a perception called time. But it may feel good as a choice in the illusion, but it is not, for there is no either–or really; it is all happening at once and timeless; all of the seeming possibilities of your Infinite nature and idea. We will speak more of this in "You Are not a Singularity." This may seem like a lot, and that, what does it really matter? I am saying this to support that knowing really who you are, what is real and only real, and what is your creation are key to everything that you experience while in this persona and world. For who you are is the all, and all that is real.

There is a phrase that goes like this: I am Spirit having a human experience. And it often refers to the experience before you that may seem challenging. That phrase is certainly just fine, but if it stops there, to me it is like being stuck in truth and descriptions and never being in the reality, your true reality of you. So, to say, "I am Spirit having a human experience and having it unlimitedly," would then be to experience who you really are playing and experiencing the part of the illusion of limitation, of being human. The point is to experience you and who you really are in and as the illusion, AND what is your natural state of being, unlimitedly and infinitely abundant in every way.

I am free, free as in this body and visual form. Free in all my expression as I am, I am free in every way possible, and that is unlimitedly possible. I am free of all description, every single one. Every one created and every description yet to be shown.

As Romeo said, and creatively I paraphrase, "But soft, what beauty I am; not as far off, but set within the view of all light to see my face of love. I know what light through yonder window breaks. It is I; it is my Love, oh how I know that it is." For I am free of all descriptions, for that which appears to be, I am not; yet, I am in that which appears to be. And so very well and good it is.

This is in line, as in the question that I state in the preface, "Are you in cause and effect, or are you of cause and effect?" The other part that I stated is the first part of a Sufi saying, "Be in the world but not of the world." (It is often thought that this quote is from the Bible, but it is actually paraphrased from scriptures as in John 17:14–16.) So, if you believe that things are real, you are not only in cause and effect but putting your unlimited power of belief in that you are of cause and effect and subject to all its laws. Understand what that means: you are in the belief that you are ruled by the laws of the universe, people, places, things and limited to them. This means you are living according to the belief that you are finite and that your reality is not of your true infinite nature and being. This is what knowing what is real and what is not is about. If any *thing* were real, then yes, you should live according to its limitations. But you are not a *thing*, you are not of the illusion, or made or born from the illusion. Who you really are is the illusion's creator. It is in your joy to claim all that you are here and all of the infinite power of your belief that you have put into the illusions—your world. That you have bowed to believing that any *thing* has a power of its own, and it is not your power. Infinite cannot ever be subject to cause and effect, for that is of time and space. In other words, you can only fool yourself into believing that any *thing* other than you has power. You convince yourself that you are subject to the descriptions and that you are limited, when the absolute reality and Truth is that you are unlimited and infinite and subject to no *thing*. All is by you, and subject, to you.

I am going to give this example of thought that you may find very easy to relate to.

There is no defense against a lie. Because in reality there is no defense; as there is no reality of need to be defensive.

Once you put out a defense to a lie you give it the power it never had. You give it the reality it is not. You give it your power. Then the illusion that is powerless on its own, and is not real, sits there in its imaginary state and grows with every moment of defense that you apply to it, until it becomes at the very least, a monster of possible belief. And at the very most an unlimited believed power that controls reality and is reality. This is what attention and conscious belief does to that which is not real; never was real, and never could be real – The Lie.

This is the very paradigm and paradox of the illusion of humanity and all things. This is the essence of the illusion of our believed existence. This is the fruit and the believed power of the concept of the tree of the knowledge of good and evil in the Garden of Eden. It is the very fabric of the power of the illusion of what is called physical reality.

It is like the old adage: What came first, the chicken or the egg? The answer in reality is that none of them came first, because the egg isn't real any more than the chicken. So it is, there need not be a defense, because the given perception being presented is completely made up. The only thing that is real and the power is believing. The reality is not what you believe, but simply who you are, and that is that you are the believer.

The very attention, awareness, and conscious belief gives a created illusion that is not real, power to appear as reality back to your attention, awareness, and consciousness. It is an amazing cycle. It is an amazing power to believe. So it is simply to know and understand that what you believe is not any power, but that you the believer, as who you actually are, is.

Remember as was written that Jesus said, "The Kingdom of God is within you; If you have seen me, you have seen the Father [the Unlimited and Infinite only One] I and the Father are one." This is you, your unchanging Reality. You are the Creator of your world, the one who knows, who believes; it is *who* you are and cannot be altered in any way. Who you are is free to fly, unlimitedly. This is Ownership.

ADDITIONAL LETTERS OF CONSCIOUSNESS

1/27/10

8:43p.m.

I am not without you; you are not without me. Dempsey, feel your creation here. Don't try to fix it; don't try to solve it. It is yours. It is not a life outside of you. This is yours to know, all who you are here. It is a creation all of consciousness, complete of you. As I have said and reminded you, it is you and only you who is creator in this, your world. All that is important; all is to feel who you are. This is that that I am. Know I am completely you. All is made by this you consciousness. Recognize you, your power in this illusion, in all illusion. All you feel, all of it, is only your infinite power.

This is your creation that is brought up before you by yourself I am. I am not limited; do you see this? You are not limited. We are not two here, simply one. And the "we" is not the reality but an understanding of myself, revealing I am. I am one and all; you are one and only one. This is the only one, the I, I am. Feel it so very real and deeply, for it is all that is real, that you can feel.

10:09p.m.

Relax, my Dempsey, my joy, relax in who you are. I am this you, no matter what. So, what else is there to want, to need, to be? What do you want to be? Know you can be what you are, who you are, who I am, for this

I am. I am your all, the all. I am; and there is no Thing else. See me through your eyes. Know this, allow this so real, so deep. Claim this that you are, that has been hidden from you. Receive me unto you, you unto yourself.

1/28/10

1:11a.m.

    I am always speaking through you, to you. This is your own special time of what I am and who you are. It is about your belief, your ability to stand in this that I am in and completely as you. Yes, trust is certainly a part of it, but feeling what you know to be, what is true, what is real, is as much set with you, before you. I know that you want to leap into your all knowing of who you are. Rest with this, and allow all else to fall away. And it will, but not as you being a sideline observer. You are interactive here. And when I say interactive, I mean inner-active. Nothing happens without you here. Like I've said in this, our beginning of your listening, the whole beach and every grain of sand are not quite right without you. You are so central to your world, your creations. You are the reason for all. My expansion of who you are that I am is everything here.

    Allow, Dempsey, allow. It is your work, your power, your process of growth in awareness of just who I am as you. It is of finite, living infinitely. I, you, being here unchained, unencumbered by appearances around us. You know intellectually that I of me is you I am. And you are gaining more knowing in depth that you feel this, see this as a reality.

    But, will you dive off the illusion into the nothing and find out, regardless of feelings of fear and doubt? Will you feel even that fear and call it your power, your hidden beliefs, and know that everything that you feel about any Thing is solely created by you? That which I am is all you. Feel all that is here now; feel it my dear one. All is well, all is really so well, for every Thing is about you. This is the moment of your truth, my reality as and for you. I am so with you here. Trust me totally to guide, protect, and keep you perfectly well and in your absolute good, my good. Every Thing is about me as you. Every *thing* is in your favor for infinite being—everything.

    I am really telling you fully that I love you, and I will finish this here with you to your wonderful loving life, and this life is for your joy, which I am so joyous in. There is a beauty here that cannot be described but simply felt and deeply known. Walk with me and in me, and you will see.

3/1/10

11:14 p.m.

It is good and well that you come to me, that which you so truly are here. Willing in this your expression of life of all. Take this time and listen. It serves you well, for everything that needs to be heard in this moment you are saying, feeling, being. And I am this you, your moment. There is never a lie of who you are as what is being felt in, and through you. It is to discern what you feel. It is the language of beyond. Allow fully, my son, my love. Feel all this here, and in this, know who you are, for this is who I am.

3/2/10

When I say you are my way, I am not secluding myself. When I say rest in me, I am not secluding you and who you are. There is a place of recognition here, this you I am. When I say come to me, it is with full thought that I am within, that I am all you in this realm that you know and call earth.

When I say peace be still, I am telling you not only what peace truly is, but that which is your true self and place of being. There is never something to reach for here; it is always the truest, most obvious, and natural state of being.

You are operating in this illusion, this your world. I am saying, supporting, and praising you to take full and complete ownership of what is you, this I am.

When I say rest, I am saying there is no Thing for you to give attention and struggle to. Not to rest, because you need to conserve your strength or because I'll do the battle for you. There is no battle; there is no Thing to struggle against or with. It is always the easiest path that is your reality. This is what these words of truth are signing you toward: this, your effortless, all infinite, unlimited true reality. Know this here who I am, this so precious and unencumbered you, without a single limit of any kind.

I am not somehow mistaken here as you, Dempsey my son, on this and in this plane of world and all illusion. I don't give you these words for some thought that is less than all me. When I say word, or thoughts of knowing to you, it is to illuminate the simple, the obvious. It is not tricky.

11:45p.m.

What if I were to tell you that you are the power of your entire world? Would you hold yourself to that? Would you see everything differently? Would you believe in who you truly are? Would you know I am you for real and you are me? Would you claim all as your creation unreservedly, without conditions of appearances? Would you, my love, live knowingly without limits or fear of any Thing? Will you honor who and what you are here, my cherished one? See this your magnificence here. Yes, right here. I am not being, as you would say, cavalier here. This is rock core to all I am. This you is all I am.

I have not confined you as me. Better yet, I have not confined me; no, not as you. See you right here that I am not limited. You are free, this unlimited and free. There is nothing, not a single power of a Thing outside of you, in all your world, in all you are, in all this here, you I am. Your experience of appearances does not determine you. Claim them for what they are, and know your power unto yourself.

I am speaking through you, as you, because I am you. All this is yours to receive unto you. I can do this in my vast, endless, and infinite being. And I do so, because it simply pleases me here to do so. It is really that plain and simple. You are me, my life. It may be stretching what you believe in your illusion of appearing circumstances, but that is the wonder and pleasure I have here to do so. It is. So let all be; relax. And if you have to, trust, and you will see what I tell you here to be absolutely true here; yes, even right here and right now. Simply know, no matter what, that all, absolutely all is of you, is your creation, your power set into the appearance of motion.

Claim it as you are doing; it is yours to do. I know at times you wonder what you are doing here. I tell you, you are expanding that I am. Expanding, not in a way that you are acquiring more, but seeing, feeling, understanding who you are in this place right now, right here. This is my joy to do so.

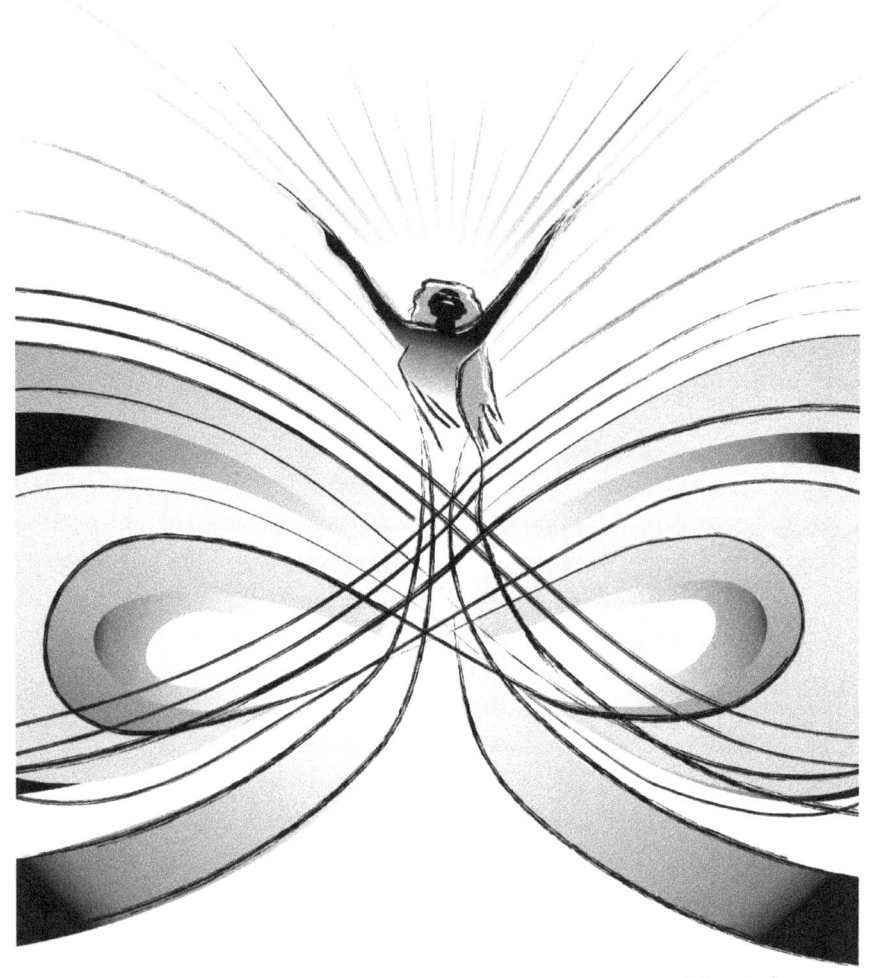

WALKING ON WATER

Will you walk on water? You certainly don't have to. But the question is will you? Not could you or can you? But the reality is, it is who you are. But will you see this as so? And then the final question. If you could, if you will, when are you willing to? Just for your understanding, I am not talking about the illusion of water called H_2O, although there really is no difference. But, do stay with me, and we will get to all of that.

As most know, this idea and concept, whether one has any religious affiliation, comes from one place and one place only, and that is in a biblical story of the New Testament, when It speaks of the man Jesus walking on water.

Let us just refresh ourselves with this story as it is told. This I will convey in its entirety from the Interlinear Bible (Matt. 14:24–32). "But the boat was now in the middle of the sea, tossed by the waves, for the wind was contrary.

"But in the fourth watch of the night, Jesus went out to them, walking on the sea. And seeing him walking on the sea, the disciples were troubled, saying, 'It is a ghost!' And they cried out from the fear.

"But immediately Jesus spoke to them, saying, 'Be comforted! I AM! Do not fear.'

"And answering him, Peter said, 'Lord, if it is You, command me to come to You on the waters.'

"And he said, 'Come!' And going down from the boat, Peter walked on the waters to go to Jesus. But seeing the strong wind, he was afraid, and beginning to sink, he cried out, 'Lord, save me!' And immediately stretching out the hand, Jesus took him, and said to him, 'Little-faith, why did you doubt?' And coming into the boat the wind ceased."

Here we have the basic story of Jesus walking on water. First of all, why is this a great story? The reason, very simply, is that it is known and understood that if you step on water, the pure physics of that action says that you will sink to whatever depths the laws of your weight and mass will keep you buoyant. This is known as the Archimedes Principle. This man, Archimedes, has been called the greatest mathematician of ancient times (298 B.C.–212 B.C.). I won't go into the full story, but he was asked to figure out a way that he could tell whether the gold crown of King Hieron of Syracuse was actually pure gold. He discovered that, using a lump of gold that weighed the same as the crown, he could know how much gold content the crown had by measuring the water it displaced. Long story short, he realized this concept one day as he entered one of the hot tubs, and the water rose when his body entered the tub. I mention all of this because it was a great discovery and a realized law that stands to this day. It is the reason a boat will float.

The weight of the object must be less than the weight of the mass of water displaced. In other words, if the weight of a boat is less than the weight of the water that a boat is displacing, the boat will float. There is an upward force of the water, because the water has weight due to its density and mass. An object will simply float when the water displaced is greater than the downward force and weight of the boat. Wow! I made that as simple as I could.

OK, we know that if we step into a volume of water like a pool or the ocean, we will, for the most part, sink. We know this simply by experience and an undeniable fact of physics that supports this principle. And let me just say that buoyancy is a law only because gravity and electromagnetism is a law of physics and the Universe. They are all seemingly undeniable laws that we simply know and accept without question.

So, for Jesus to walk on this windy choppy sea, let alone Peter to be able to walk on the water for any amount of time, was contradictory to all the laws of buoyancy, gravity, and electromagnetism, let alone the fact that these are some of the core building blocks of the Universe. Get that: it was not possible, according to the laws of physics that govern this illusion of physical world. And yet, the quantum of the physics even muddies the water and stirs up the pot of this illusion that any of these laws could be true and have consistency. According to quantum physics, nothing stays in any solid condition. Particles and atoms literally pop in and out of known existence. As I have said before, quantum physics does not work according to the same laws of any known natural physics such as buoyancy.

This is much more than the mere concept of a person walking on water. It goes much further and says so much more. This is important for the conveyance and allegory of thought and understanding ahead.

If you have not guessed or surmised by now, this is going to be about challenging the beliefs, perceptions, and the accepted knowledge of what is actually possible and the assumed reality. Your infinite unlimited and unconditional reality.

And yes, I do address this perceived reality of universe: nothing is actually real. But there is something in this concept and story that is greatly supportive to encourage and strengthen this knowing and reality.

It is all about standing firm in what is real, what is reality, and who you are as what is only and always reality.

Before I go into anything else here, I am going to present something of an experience that has come up for me, and I simply am inspired to express it now to you. It is a writing that I did for myself when I was feeling a lot of power to claim unto me, and I recognized that I had to write it down to allow and feel what it was that I was feeling. And this is how it went.

I write this not for anyone. I don't even really feel I know at this time really why I write this for me, but I know that I do. What I feel is so deep and almost incomprehensible, except that it feels so endlessly, senselessly confusing.

I stand in the trust here of what I know. That is, that what I know is thus far seemingly the best and maybe all that can be known. And yet I call unto myself, for there is not another to call unto myself. There is not another to call unto but that which I am. This that I feel feels like death of all I see and physically know in my world. Do I think that these words will ever have meaning? And what could really matter as reality here?

I do continue to claim all that I am, all that I feel as my power. I have no other knowing to do here. I feel no other absolute reality as the truth. I have simply trusted that which I am as all that really is, and I take one step as it comes after another.

I feel the questioning of myself, my reality, and continue to allow the feeling and let the illusion of story go. I discover in doing so that I have so much belief of my power in the many supporting belief structures of and in my world. I could then say that I surrender to what I feel like as unto death, but then call it my power and know that there is not a better option but to embrace it as my power in my creation. I have to let go of how I have predisposed how it should look or how I should feel. I come to the acceptance and understanding that this is how my power feels: very indescribably powerful. And that it is by my design to call unto myself in my creations all that I am.

I am that which I am; and I shall let it play and prove its self out to me as what is real is only real. What is only real is always real and changes not. I am infinite and unlimited regardless of appearances. In this I do trust, because I realize that this is what I know.

Regardless of the winds and stormy seas, and all appearances and seeming laws of man and nature, I walk knowing all is perfect, absolutely perfect to the smallest fragment in appearances, perfect. I also dare to trust what I know until I trust because I know. I am willing to be the real-life experiment and prove as me what is reality and real, and who I am. I will start in the experience of my unconditional belief.

Not waiting for something outside of who I am, not some prayer, some sign to convince me or compel me to trust and be the proof. I cannot shake from me what I know; it has not come from outside of me but from within. This knowing cannot be altered, only set in the illusion's fire and claimed and refined as undeniable within that which I am. In this is the claiming and releasing of my power back to me. As I said before, resist nothing, for infinite is just that, infinite, and stand in this that I am. What is actually real cannot for any reason, for anything, be altered or changed. So, I am reunited with my power in that I accept, feel, and recognize my power and essence of all I am. Consciousness in an expanded reality that I am, that I always really am.

There is no Thing to resist. Not a Thing to take seriously but unlimited joy, love, and infinite freedom to feel as my experience. So, I am at rest and so very free.

This is what I wrote as an avenue to allow and open up unto my true self. Again, I must say as unto myself, the laws of man and the Universe are not real. These are only belief structures, the image of the idea, my idea.

CHOICE

When you think of choice, you might think also of free will. And, in this relationship of choice to free will, you might call this your individual power of being. The more choices that you have, the more freedom of options you could feel that you have and are capable of having. But remember, sometimes what we believe and think of as real is an illusion to fool infinite and unlimited Consciousness; yes, you. For, in duality, it feels empowering to have any manipulation of control at your disposal, but it is part of the illusion. You may feel and think of this control and power of will as the reality. So, follow me down the rabbit hole, and see how far it goes.

I spoke and wrote of consequences not being real but, rather, a created belief to hold consciousness in the belief of duality being real. This is actually a cycle, because the belief in any *thing* being real creates the belief in consequences. I want to point out here that choice and decisions were also a creation at the beginning and born from duality, being in the same cycle of the illusion of your creation being of its own and real. (As with duality, I am not saying that the illusion of choice is bad.)

But there was the belief in the story of the beginning in Genesis, that Adam and Eve had a decision to make about not taking of the fruit of the Tree of Good and Evil, or taking of it and suffering the consequences of dying. In reality, or as I call it, outside of duality, there was no real tree, no Good and Evil, and no decision that needed to be made. It was a conscious creation in and of Consciousness by Consciousness, as one of the deeper props to hold and convince Consciousness that the illusion was real. Consciousness was not only in the illusion but believed that it was the illusion, separate from what it really was. Thus, the masterpiece of duality was created, with so many supporting brushstrokes on the canvas of the created idea.

As I have said, what was created was the illusion that there could be anything real but the One Infinite Consciousness. This that is the illusion of the possibility of another that is known as duality. So, the Thing called the tree wasn't real. Good and Evil that was based in choice and opposing sides and powers aren't real. And, whether to partake of the fruit, with the consequences of disobeying, was never and is never real. There is never a choice—an either-or decision—to make, unless one thinks that something is real and that there is a good-bad or better or worse choice to make.

So, when you believe in and live by choice, that you need to be making the best or right decisions, you are supporting that your creation the illusion is real. You are not only believing that your free will of choice is your power, but you are also believing that what you believe is your power. It is not what you believe that is the power, but simply, that you are the one and only believer and there is not another. Believing that anything is actually real and has any power of its own holds you in the illusion of limitation. I am saying here that when you put the power of your belief in what you choose, you are re-shackling, or simply adding more chains of belief that you are of limitation, instead of the true, effortless nature of your being that you are unconditionally unlimited and infinite. Again, there are no consequences. Consequences are a creation of believing duality to be real.

There is nothing more important than standing on the knowing and understanding that absolutely *nothing* is real, *ever*, and that all is created by You-Consciousness. All is merely an absolute illusion.

You see, feeling that you have the power to change something by the choice that you make is simply a lie, because it entraps you in the belief that anything is real. It only keeps you in a three-dimensional world and thought, and bound to people, places, things, and circumstances. In other words, you are calling them real and putting your infinite, unlimited, creative, conscious power into the illusion. You are then not trusting, believing, and knowing who you really are. Choice is in and born from duality and is masked as the power, all to convince you that you need to control and change reality to keep you safe and well. The only power is you believing and knowing your natural state of reality and being that creates every *thing*.

As duality was a creation, so was and is choice. Again, I am not saying that the illusion of choice is bad, no more than I am saying that duality is bad. Your joy is to experience and play in both, without putting power into them. But, to believe in choice as the power, or duality as the power, is to believe that the illusion is real. What may seem as a choice is really a reflection of your belief and who you believe you are. In other words, if you believe you are limited, that who you are is just a creation. Any *thing* that you have put your power and belief into to make you think that it is real will have consequences, judgment, and power in your world. You will convince your true self that making the proper choice is what is needed to keep you from a result that you prefer not to have as a believed experience.

As I have said, it is not what you believe that is the glory and the power, or what is real. It is simply that you are the one and only believer in your world. In this creative process, you are completely unlimited. Take that in. I bring this up again, because it is also so with choice. It is not what you choose that is the power and what is real. The only thing that is real is that you believe unconditionally; You-Consciousness is the one believing, and this believing appears in the illusion in duality as choice. But it really is not. In a simple, concise thought of understanding, I will say that your belief is not from and of the appearance and power of choice. So, if you believe the illusion of duality to be real, you will believe in choice being real and your power. But, the appearance and illusion of choice is in and of your unlimited power of unconditional belief. Your infinite and unlimited freedom is not in the limiting and binding chains of choice and its consequences. Your freedom comes from your infinite and natural state of joy in and of no limitations.

The illusion of being limited is created when you believe in any one *thing* as reality. I will offer more expression and understanding of this in "You Are not a Singularity."

Let that soak in with you for now. You might be thinking, what does this have to do with what I have titled "Walking on Water?" It is about letting go of beliefs and created belief structures that you have called your power and real. Keep walking with me and allow. Remember, what you read here is really unto yourself, and it will all be purposeful and supportive.

What is your infinite joy in un-limitation is that which only looks like a choice in duality. This unconditional and unlimited joy is not attached to agendas, outcomes, or any *thing* being real. When you follow your joy, it is in deep appreciation for all of your creations or it could not be in your unconditional joy. You have created every *thing* and everyone in your world, and creating them as appearing to be separate and real is truly an amazing, fantastic accomplishment. Remember, every single *thing* that you feel and experience is your power, or you could not ever possibly feel it.

When I have said that you are the only power in your world, you really are. Hear that again: you are the only power in your world, ever. There is never a mistake that you can ever make. It is not possible. Remember, it is all and only an illusion that you have created for the experience of your joy of your unconditional, unlimited self. You are always only unto yourself, and you are creating every *thing* absolutely perfectly, as you have designed it to be for your joy in your human experience

Stay with me here. Soak that in. I am certain that more will open up as we continue further down the rabbit hole. Just simply stay firm on the foundation that absolutely nothing is real.

Trust what is unfolding to you as we walk along, and allow as you already have. Remember, trust and know that you are always unto your very self.

What you have seen is that in the belief that duality is real are varying attributes, such as a creation and belief in responsibility. In this belief of responsibility being real is the belief in Consequences. In that, is the belief that any *thing* is real, which creates the belief of choice being real and a need and power to reason. To support that the illusion is real and requires judgment, again holding You-Consciousness in the belief that any *thing* is actually real. These are just some of the attributes that, in turn, play major supporting roles of Conscious power in believing that your world is real, with a power of its own.

These attributes that I mentioned in the preceding paragraph are instrumental, in one way or another. Your feelings of consequences, responsibility, a need for choice and reasoning all pop up your hidden beliefs to you and give appearance in your world. You feel and experience them in people, places, things, and circumstances. Your belief that is your all-powerful creative process creates an illusion of its idea of a *thing*, power, and life outside of you. It is so magnificently created, it can convince you to believe in it as the reality.

Believing that reasoning is your power is to call the singularity of a circumstance real. Reasoning about right and wrong, justice, fairness, or any *thing* simply means that you have your power in a *thing*.

You can understand something for your pure joy of seeing how it came about as an illusion. But to try to figure something out to change it or call it a power is to keep your essence and power hidden in the singular illusion of a *thing*.

With all of these created beliefs, choice is tied in as a major supporting role to convince Consciousness that any *thing* is actually real. Your belief in the illusion of duality being real puts you in the belief that the illusions of responsibility, consequences, and reasoning are real. As soon as you put your conscious belief in choice as your power, you are caught in the belief that there is a possible right or wrong choice. It is almost like the back door to believing in every one of those beliefs of duality being real again and putting your power back into them. This will simply say to you that you have more of your unlimited power remaining to claim from them as you feel more being triggered in your experience being brought up to you. Wow! That is a lot. But, it is what is real. I am saying to notice this belief in choice that supports any *thing* being real. Know who you are: Consciousness creating every *thing* in your entire world. Reclaim your power from a choice being your power and reality. Every time that you believe something is real, you are actually in the belief of choice. You choose something because you believe the illusion before you to be real.

Because nothing is real, there can be no optimum or right and wrong choice. It is always You-Consciousness believing in the expression of your joy that gives the illusion of choice. This belief in choice holds your Infinite and Unlimited Self in the singular finite illusion that what you see before you as your experience is your reality. Again, this will open up more in the chapter "You Are not a Singularity."

All of these beliefs are still your power creating a fantastic illusion, no matter what it looks like. Remember, there is no bad belief. I am simply saying to know that you are the only believer in your world, creating and/or believing something to be real when it is not. All of these beliefs from and in duality are supporting roles that play a part in convincing you that you are less than you infinitely really are. Remember, it all had to be created so that Consciousness, who you really are could even be in the part of limitation and there being another.

When in the story Peter stepped out of the boat onto the choppy and windy sea, it was not by choice but from the belief that Jesus the Christ was who he said he was.

In the story, the disciples did not recognize Jesus in the storm and on the water. So, Peter asked, Matt. 14:28, "'If it is you command me to come to you on the waters.'" Jesus represented the power of Infinite Consciousness. And so it is with you. Keep trusting who you know you are until you trust because you know who you are. Be the experiment of your knowing, and trust who you are.

We will continue with this story and what I mean by singularity, but first, I am going to connect with you on and in feelings and experiences. All of this is in and about Ownership and your True Self and unlimited freedom.

YOUR FEELINGS, YOUR EXPERIENCE

Understand that when you think that you are looking out, or outside of yourself, you are really looking within. This is an absolute that cannot change. I said that everything that you feel, everything that you experience, is your power or you could not even possibly feel it. To elaborate on that a bit, I would also say that you couldn't feel it or *know it*. Your feelings are how you know and recognize your essence and power in this world. When I say feelings and experiences, I am not talking about judging from them that any *thing* is actually real. They are actually signs and triggers of your very Conscious power, reflecting back to you, within you. They are catching your attention, telling you to take notice.

They are saying, look, right here is your belief, your power, your very essence of consciousness. You are totally meant to experience all of your life as you design it to be.

Your absolute reality is always staring you straight in the face, hiding in plain view, the very reality that is what and who you are. It is the reality that you are experiencing. You are experiencing you as the power of conscious belief being felt. As the saying goes, the proof is in the pudding. I am saying that you are your own proof. It is all about you, and you must know that you are the experiment. You are your own blessing. The simple truth that every *thing* that you see, every *thing* that you feel, all of your five senses, every *thing* is all happening, expressed, and experienced within you. Your very body is an experience within. You experience your body within your consciousness, and your inner feelings direct your attention to that. Your whole world and Universe is your conscious experience within, this that you really are. Nothing is actually outside of you.

You are not aware of it anywhere but within you. Through your feelings, Consciousness, which is all you are, shouts out to you who you are and where and who reality is. It's you, the real you. There is only ownership. It is not changeable in anyway. The entire Kingdom is within you and is you.

As was said earlier, you are meant to experience and know all your life, and to experience all of it, you have to feel all you feel as your power—because it is. To experience it absolutely unshackled, free, and unlimited. Can you imagine joyfully feeling everything that you feel in your world and experience without being guarded, or worried about consequences or harm? Can you imagine really knowing and calling it your power and feeling that as such? Feeling everything that you feel and knowing there is nothing that is real but the wonderful power that you are experiencing within you? You have created every *thing*. Take a moment to feel that and know that. It is absolute, unlimited, unconditional joy, love, and freedom. It is who you really are and your absolute natural state of being. You don't need to earn it or work for it in any way. You are the Unlimited Infinite one in your world. This is your reality, your ownership. This is truly being in the world but not of the world. It is what is, and what only is real. You are welcoming, claiming, discovering, revealing you unto yourself. This is absolute bliss; this is unconditional freedom. Being no longer hidden but revealed is what is referred to as enlightenment. It is simply all of who you are. Feel all of you.

Know that you can make no mistakes, no matter what illusions of judgments and consequences are created from your Conscious belief that has made a circumstance or a *thing* to seem so real and outside of you.

You don't try to change any *thing* to change your feelings or make them stop. You fully, or at least as fully as you possibly can, acknowledge the power from any *thing* that you are feeling, no matter how enormous it may feel. Acknowledging the circumstance that triggered the feeling may hold your belief still in the illusion and call it real. I find it best to simply call the *thing* that triggered your feelings, your created illusion, and feel the power from your feelings. Claim it as what is real and the only power that you are actually feeling back to you. When you are willing to feel what you feel, whether it is favorable or unfavorable, you are loving and appreciating your very true self. If you later want to look at the circumstance you created that brought up your power to you, after you have claimed enough of your power of belief that it was real, you may do that. But not to judge it, figure it out, or to call it real, but to simply see how you crafted such a fantastic illusion. If you do find yourself wanting it to change or judge it, simply feel that and claim more of you, your essence, your power back to who you really are.

I am bringing up the feeling of wanting to change things in relationship to this story. Notice that Jesus didn't try to stop or change the strong winds and the stormy seas. He let it be. He knew who he was and that it was not real. Changing the circumstances simply was not a requirement in the equation to step out and walk on the water. What is really special here is that he knew who he was and what was real. He claimed all of that and his power by stepping onto the water. He claimed all he was and that there was no power but him, or over him, with and in every step that he took.

What is really noticeable is that when he finished his walk and reached where his joy was taking him, he entered the boat, where at that moment, the wind and seas completely calmed. It is a natural thing to take place when you claim your power from any circumstance. Whether that be the illusion of limited love, relationships, money, health, or anything else, none of it can stay in its present form and singular appearance of power. When Robert Scheinfeld speaks of this in *Busting Loose*, he says, "However it looks it looks." Changing *things* is never the reason that you claim who you are and your power, your true essence unto yourself. *It was never real anyway.* Having the hologram You created by Your power change, is more like a side effect. It is never the purpose. You are never choosing a singular *thing* to be a certain way. You simply know who you are and follow your joy, and your joy follows you.

Absolutely everything that you feel and experience is your unconditional unlimited power; everything, or there would not be a possibility for you to experience and feel it. It is your belief; it is you the believer. There is nothing that you feel outside of you, as there is never any power outside of who you are. You are really always the only power in your world and always unto yourself. Take your walk, know who you are, and claim all that you feel as your power. Be the experiment. Welcome all you feel with open heart and arms. Let what is real and who is real prove themselves unto you and as you. Jesus said to his followers, Matt. 14:27, "'Be comforted I AM.'" It is a statement of reality, of who you really are, who and what I am. There is never a command, rule, or law proposed to achieve something that you are not or to become more. Comforted is your natural state of Be-ing. Knowing who you are and experiencing all you are is your greatest comfort. It is your very being. It is your very I am.

Now, we are going to take a journey into something a little deeper, which we have been talking about relating to your creative process and claiming and taking back your power. Ready? Here we go.

YOU ARE NOT A SINGULARITY

In all of this, I am speaking of who you really are, infinite and unlimited. In this, know that infinite is not a number or amount. It is not a quantity or number that keeps going and never ends. Infinite is not linear. Trying to comprehend that, just like trying to comprehend that there is really nothing, is not really possible to describe. There is no reference point for it to be articulated as a *thing*, let alone a concept of real understanding. But, I will give it some expression. As I said, infinite is not linear in any way. Infinite is infinitely dimensional. It has no starting point, no ending point, and is not an endless continuation of a *thing*. When I say that infinite is infinitely dimensional, I am conveying it like a single dot but without conception of borders. It is not imaginable or describable. So, there is never a crevasse, crack, dot, strip, or other spot where it is not or that it is not all there is. I say that in really linear terms in the attempt to feel what infinite is. This is exactly why Consciousness is all there is, all and only power, and all complete knowing. I am saying this because you, this real you, is this very Infinite One.

What I present to you is that you are not a particular singularity. This singularity is what I said in earlier chapters I would discuss later. It is very important to why you claim your power instead of trying to create something. Remember, this is to expand your concept of who you are and your freedom, to support you in releasing the belief that the illusion needs to be controlled, and that you are not a *thing* and finite. Who you really are cannot be comprehended in time and space, even though you are in your created illusion of time and space. Yes, you actually are infinite and unlimited. Here, I want to bring out the thought of the belief in infinite possibilities and what that worded description says. What is framed in the expression of possibilities is a word that indicates and points to the option of choices. And infinite possibilities are infinite choices.

In those choices is the option to have one thing be over another. Or, have them all available but waiting to be implemented. So, when you choose one of your infinite possibilities to be your reality, you have chosen a belief and construct of limitation.

I can hear some of my friends right now saying, "Ya, Dempsey, but it is what I want. Why can't I have that?" You actually do, and none of it is real anyway, because all infinite actualities are yours and your idea. It is good to know what you are really wanting when you say that you have a desired outcome. First of all when you say that you want something you are saying that you don't have it and that you lack it. You are also saying that you recognize what it is that you want or you could not even have the consciousness and awareness to want it. It is important here to really understand what you are saying when you say that you want any *thing*. You may believe that you want something, be it person, place, or thing. What you are actually wanting out of any particular *thing* is a feeling that you believe it will give you. No matter what it is that you want there is an end result feeling of your personal good that is the outcome. This outcome is experienced as a believed feeling. This believed feeling directly supports who you think you are in many ways. First of all, there is nothing that is not your Consciousness. Since you can only feel your power and essence, this is really what you believe you don't have and are separated from. Every feeling that you have and want represents your experience. This is simply because you can't even feel and experience what you want unless you know the feeling first to want it. All you are ever in reality wanting is the experience of who you really are. All you ever really want is the experience of your infinite joy of your being, even in this singularity. You actually know who you really are. Your essence in reality is actually all you really want to feel and experience. You simply are Infinite Consciousness, and your real joy is in your own recognition. The only thing that you can possibly experience is your essence, your Consciousness, your power, and your belief. You *can* have the *thing* or person that you think is going to give you what you want, and still never be satisfied. Just to keep in mind: there is never a circumstance or *thing* that actually creates the feeling of your power that you want. It is always just the opposite. Your power creates the circumstance and thing that you believe that you are feeling your power as. You may mistake your joy as being what you want, believing that your joy comes from what you want. What you think you want can only be a reflection of your joy, that is your creative power believing. What you are really recognizing that you want in reality is the experience of your essence and power. Understand you can't feel anything else but your consciousness, your essence, and belief, because you are the believer in your world, and that is all there is. Wanting what you want is wonderful. Simply know that the only thing that you are really wanting is your experience of who you really are. The only thing that you have ever felt and experienced, or could possibly ever experience, is who you really are. What you believe and what you are feeling about is not your power. It is all about your feelings that represent your experience, that represent your Consciousness, your Infinite Self. You are never lacking or actually wanting. This is the reality, because, You are simply not a Singularity. Stay with me here, as we really take a journey down the rabbit hole. Whee!

If you haven't felt or thought of this already, when you choose any one *thing* to be your joy and freedom, you have actually entrapped yourself in a cage of limitation. And when I say choose any one *thing*, I am saying believe it as your reality, as who you are, as a real and actual power. You are really saying who you feel you are and that you are less than the unlimited and infinite that you really are.

Possibilities are a perception from and in duality of people, places, and things being real. It does denote a very linear world, even though you use the word "infinite" before possibilities.

This is where this gets interesting. You see, nothing, absolutely nothing, is real. It is all within You, You-Consciousness. You are infinite with an infinite idea. That idea is what you know, and this knowing is Consciousness believing infinitely. Let that soak in a bit. I have a special letter of consciousness that I received along this topic that I will now share with you.

8/28/10

10:32a.m.

"I am understanding, breathing, knowing, and being this very you as I am; this you are. Realizing that I am only. That the very one and only you I am. Not one in your own separation of individual persona, but all one I am in all your reality of who you are I am. Who you really, really are. Realize this true, for it always is. I am only and fully.

Rest in the moment of all nothing; it is infinite and unlimited, as all and only power. Get this as you, yourself, Unlimited and only power. There is your reality here, as all power can only be only power; and only power infinitely is always unlimited. It is not something to create to see, to be; it simply is without variance or reason of any question to be different I am.

You have, you do, and you will allow in this you know, that all you I am. I cannot be separated as all you I so fully am. No Thing else is real, no Thing else has volition, no Thing else is any power in any way of any kind. Only you that I wonderfully am. Joy, and rejoice again, over and over, without end, I do here as this place called you. Grasp this I am, a little more in you fully, joy I am here. Rest in that I am not a Thing, and no Thing is that I as you did not allow and create, for all is only as I am; only fully as you are all I am. I am never less with you; for this you I am beyond any number to possibly measure. Yes, you Infinite is really Infinite without end. Rest in Nothing being indescribably all there is. You I perfectly am.

1:10p.m.

I am not a singularity; you are not a singularity. I am all being and infinitely so. You are all being, now and infinitely so as this I am. There is not a surplus of all I am or all you are. It is all as it were taking place now as in time but not, and certainly not of time as perceived to be. All is so very simple and plain, when the curtain of time and its collaborator space are taken away.

When I say infinite is infinite, it has nothing to do with time as in lasting forever. It is all about an incomprehensible being-ness of you I am. Everything infinitely of my idea is not only now and possible, it is so. So, what I am saying here in this unto you I am, is that all infinite possibilities are not waiting in the wings, as if they might somehow be: they are. They are not just a possible thing to be; they are, unto me, an actuality that is. It is when you get stuck on a singular particular actuality that things become burdensome, and yes, bothersome. This is where your infinite power and absolute unlimited belief gets trapped into believing that which is not so and is not real. Your power is assumed and given to a particular actuality as who you I am by the simplistic nature I am to believe. And, Infinite you are is tricked and fooled by the power you are to believe less than I am.

So, again, I am not ever a singularity, and so neither can you ever be. This is not a possibility; as I really am, this you always and only really are. This may seem strange at first glance, but possibilities are a perception in and of time, stretched in the thing called space. I am saying that my infinite idea is yours, is you, and all is before me. There is no idea that is over or before another, and it is infinitely so. And nothing, not a single infinite idea created, is of its own power and real as from its separate own self.

It is all my infinite joy to know, to be as if there could possibly be another of any kind or Thing, when only I am, this very all you infinite one. There is no way to convey infinite in finite descriptions of limitation, but it is so that you really are. You cannot have a limit, as this you are. Know this and trust, because you know who you are, I am beautifully."

So, from this there is the recognition that there are really infinite actualities. But, when seen in the holographic illusion of duality, they appear as possibilities, just as time appears to be so but is not the reality. Quantum physics has said that there even might be infinite universes. That means infinite personas of you, of me, having an infinite variation of our existence in each one. But, it is all one consciousness. Even in infinite worlds, it is all still an illusion and not real. So, what is real is not finite. It is the infinite play and idea known and believed in the One Consciousness, the all there is. This is all and only to support your freedom to think in terms that are beyond constructs and limitations. This is not to mandate a particular way in which you must approach infinite or your Infinite Self. When you think that you are lacking, you can't be. It is simply that you believe that a particular space of time and *thing* is real, and you have placed your unlimited power of consciousness in believing that an event or *thing* is what is real.

I am going to add some support to this concept of Infinite, and time and space.

The Infinite idea of "other," is known in Me-Consciousness as like unto, "the snap of the finger," and "a twinkle of an eye." Time is like the slowing down of the Infinite idea of another in order to have a perception of the idea, being in it as an expression of experience. I will explain.

All is my idea being that I am Consciousness, so I actually only and completely feel all of it, for it is one idea, - infinitely known. I am in the perception of perspectives and all of it is readily available to me.

In linear terms, time only looks like movement because of the illusion of the limiting of the Infinite idea to a singular perception. Understand that the beauty and magnificence of the illusion that is called time and space is the infinite appearing to be finite, limited, and a singular idea. It is really quite a fantastic created illusion. Just to conceptualize this and another way to say this in a description of linear terms: Time looks like movement because of the slowing down of the infinite speed. Even at that, we live in the illusion that our planet and the galaxy alone are traveling at enormous speeds, in the hundreds of thousands of miles per hour. Even the description of speed is based on the perspective of the Infinite in the finite called space and time (distance per hour).

It is all amazing and indescribably fantastic. This illusionary playground of form, which is in its self space and time, I-Consciousness have created just for me; just for me! I created it for my wonder, full of infinite joy.

Once you begin to get that there is not *another*, that there is *nothing*, that *nothing is actually happening*, all freedom of your Infinite Self is actually available. Not only is it made plain and simple that only Infinite Consciousness is all there is, but that you are that very one that only and really is.

All is only joy. All is only your infinite idea, and all of it is now available to you, to be felt at every moment, as, in, and through you. It is all your treasured experience of your Infinite Self and idea. You never feel a singularity, because there is only You, your infinite Self to experience represented by any *thing*.

The bottom line with that is when you believe a singular *thing* or anything to be real, you have fooled yourself with tremendous power to believe that you are not unlimited and the power in your world, but the finite and illusionary are.

When you claim your power from the illusion of any singular *thing* or circumstance, you are actually freeing yourself up to the infinite freedom that you actually are. Not to possibilities that could be, but infinite actualities that are. And since none of them are real, you can only be resting in infinite freedom, that which you really are. I realize that is a lot, but it is worth knowing and feeling, for you are here unto your very Infinite Self. You are feeling this, your infinite power, as if you were feeling your infinite actualities. You are feeling your Self, your infinite idea. Infinite is your experience and you are the power you experience. You feel like less when you believe a *singular thing* and actuality to be real. You are still feeling your Infinite Self and actualities, but you have believed a singular actuality to have a power of its own. This is when you are fooled to believe that what you feel is a finite power, and in this you feel and experience yourself as finite. But it simply is not actually real. It is not who you are.

It can be thought of in the story of Jesus walking on the sea, when Peter stepped out and started to sink for fear that he had somehow failed. I want to say right here that Peter was the only one who was willing and believed that he could step out and do the seemingly impossible. In the story, he was willing to be the experiment. As this story is told, he embraced who he was, even if it was for just a moment. For that moment, he was focused and trusted in the Infinite as he looked to Jesus. When he stepped onto the rough sea, he was really stepping unto his real Infinite Self. For that moment, nothing was real but his Unlimited Infinite Self. The story says that Jesus said, Matt. 14:31, "'Little-faith, why did you doubt?'" This was not a reprimand or belittlement. In Hebrew, this "little faith" is more like asking, "Why did you stop?"

You focused on the Infinite for a brief period of time. It was when Peter put his belief in the singular circumstance that the waves and wind became the reality. That is when the belief in the illusion of its consequences brought the feeling of fear. I want to point out that his feeling of fear was a strong trigger and signpost to where he had placed his infinite, unlimited power of belief. Infinite by and in its own belief, then played the part of becoming an illusion of a finite, singular idea of reality.

You are incomprehensibly infinite, and unconditionally unlimited. This is your Reality always. Step into the Reality of you, your Infinite Self. It is your journey, your walk, always your life, unlimited.

FINAL STATEMENT

This one idea that I spoke of in the beginning really culminates in this last chapter.

All that ever could be, infinitely is. It is not just a possibility. When I say that you are Infinite it is because you really are. You are not Infinite like one might think of never dying or being Eternal. It is very easy to get entranced and caught in the believed and accepted words and phrases that are used in a system of any particular language. What is over looked is that often a word, phrase, and description of thought becomes an idiom of belief. A word or phrase really has a propensity to be glazed over or limited in its meaning when it is often used in conversation or is just grammatically correct. This all said, Infinite is all and completely Infinite even though there is no *thing* to reference this to. But it can be felt and experienced. When you feel any *thing* what so ever, you are always all Consciousness experiencing You, your Infinite Self. Get this: In the mind of You-Consciousness is your Infinite Idea. You are Infinite knowing. In the one and only mind-Consciousness is this infinite idea that are all only known as actualities. There is not one thing that is not present and completely known infinitely. That is why a *possibility* is only a *representation* of the infinite idea. This is why you can only actually feel your infinite idea even when it is shown and triggered to you as a singular circumstance of possibility. All that is Real and True is your Infinite timeless Self. Time is a perception, giving a finite perspective of the infinite illusion that actually is. Nothing but you is the power and real. None of the infinite actualities are real. They are all simply like a structured idea and thought. All of them, even now, this limited and finite amount that you seem to see and experience as your world. No matter what it looks like, it is only a created known and believed idea of Consciousness. It can't have any power or reality. It is only when you as Consciousness believe *in* any idea that you see in your world that it takes on your power, because you have believed the illusion of the idea to be real. You have given your power and your life to the illusion that is your world. You and your infinite power have believed finite to be real. In doing so, you have taken one of your infinite actualities of illusion and made it seem real, making your experience of you less than infinite and creating a power to appear separate from who you are.

Instead of wanting a particular *thing* that isn't real anyway, you reclaim your power from what you have believed and felt as real. Reclaim it, knowing you created it and that it is not actually real. So, then, you live, feel and experience your infinite actualities instead of finite possibilities.

I said earlier that there is a real difference between Consciousness being the believer and Consciousness believing in something. Every *thing* that you see, every *thing* that you experience, is a finite perspective of what You-Unlimited Consciousness has infinitely believed. Consciousness believing is absolutely effortless and unlimited. Consciousness—*who* you really are, believing in some *thing*—draws you, your power, and *who* you are into it. Believing any *thing* to be real feels like effort, because you have placed your power in illusion, which really says to you that you believe your very essence to be finite and holds you in that belief and in the struggle of the illusion of duality. *You are not a singularity.*

As I have said, Truths never are an order, command, condition, or law. The Bible says, Matt: 6:33, "Seek you first the Kingdom of God and his righteousness, and all of these things will be added unto you" (or paraphrased: Look within where the Infinite reigns and see what is real as who you are; and all of the Infinite actualities of illusion are within you and subject to you and your power). But, you can't call them real and do this at the same time: it is impossible.

You are magnificent beyond understanding and words. You, *who* you really are, are really this Infinite. You are always so very free to fly; absolutely free to walk on the stormy sea. It is your Peace. It is simply *who* you always and really are.

Your feelings are the indicator of your conscious experience of your persona and your world, which in both cases is the creation of your consciousness. And in both of these cases is the experience of your power, created by you the Believer. To feel all you feel and welcome it fully is to really recognize and experience all you really are. There is no other or greater joy.

In this understanding, when you claim your conscious belief that you have put into any *thing* as being real, claim it unto yourself with open arms and heart. In other words, when you claim, claim with as much appreciation as you can for the *thing* from which you claim your power. You created it; appreciate you as creator, while you claim your power from the belief in it. It is simply much more powerful to do this than to claim with resentment for this creation of yours. Appreciation keeps you from adding any more power into it by calling it real.

You are not moving through what is known as Life. Life is moving as your experience through you and is you. There is nothing outside of who you really are. You are infinitely unlimited. Trust what you know, until you trust because you know.

Thoughts of Support:
- Resist nothing.
- Take nothing seriously.
- Everything that you feel, everything that you experience is your power, or you could not possibly feel it.
- Feel all you feel as your power, and claim it as yours.
- Your power is You-Consciousness Believing, your natural creative being.
- Appreciate what you created when you claim.
- You are always unto yourself.
- You are the only power and Creator in and of your world.
- Nothing is real but consciousness. It is who you really are, Infinite and Unlimited.
- There is only your ownership, you that is Consciousness in your world, You-Creator.

- You are not a singularity of no thing, of no kind; you are infinite.
- Trust what you know and who you are, until you trust because you know who you are.

You simply are free to fly.

Further Support:

Infinite is the absolutely unfathomable, inner and outer woven, endless, beginning-less, timeless, space-less, and incomprehensibly dimensional. I say all of this greatly using linear description. It is infinitely incomprehensible in the illusion of time and space.

How could who you really are, Infinite Consciousness and knowing, possibly hide its Self as you? It would seem in this singularity of appearing illusion to be like amnesia or something. I want to address this because it was always staring me in the face, and I just left it as incomprehensible. But, I believe that I can shed some light on this that is indescribable.

It is the very power of the believing of Consciousness that allowed Infinite to experience being a finite singularity. In short, it is your incomprehensible infinite power that allows you to experience a finite illusion of reality. It is always by the only power that is, the only power you are. It is You-Consciousness believing. This essence that you are, the believer, is power that cannot have a measure to it, and cannot be described, for it is not a *thing*. That is why Consciousness is often called Spirit.

Recognize this within yourself. Although infinite that you are cannot be comprehended as a description, it is always felt and experienced as you. It is your actual experience.

Claiming your power is really to say, that in reality, you are not ever feeling a singular point in time and space called an event or circumstance. Claiming your infinite essence and power, is to simply be in recognition that it is always your Infinite Consciousness and True Self that you feel and recognize.

There are not possibilities waiting to be created by you. It only looks that way in the illusion of time and space. So what you always are really feeling is your conscious idea of infinite actualities. Remember, nothing is real. The only thing that you really feel is your infinite idea. I say this in linear comprehensible terms. It is as if you are feeling your infinite actualities; just the same as you have thought you were feeling and only experiencing this singularity of the idea that appears before you now.

What you always feel and experience is your Self, your essence, your Infinite Idea, that is You-Consciousness. It is so fantastically, wonderfully amazing. So this is what recognizing, welcoming, and claiming your power back to you is really all about.

Prayer is simply recognition of your real Self. There is only one recognition, and that is infinitely all I am. It is in this awareness that I pray without ceasing. It is in this that I am always in meditation. I am in my own recognition. That is all; feeling all my Infinite Self not a finite singularity. Being in recognition is what I feel and experience as my amazing Infinite Self, and is the meditation. You stop feeling that you are a singularity and that you are ever really feeling a singular *thing* of space and time. As you continue claiming and are in your recognition, you eventually get to the moment that you stop believing that you are ever feeling a *thing*. You start embracing your infinite joy as what you are feeling. The believed focal point of power shifts because you are Consciousness believing.

As I said previously, I could say Consciousness knowing instead of believing but I use believing to convey a certain creative feeling of experience. So let me say it this way just to add to the perspective. You are the knower. It is not what you know that is the life, the power, and reality. Your life, power, and reality are simply that who you are is the knower. You are always in reality, fully knowing the experience of your Infinite Self. There is none other to know but you the believer.

You are the unlimited infinite power simply being in the illusion. The illusion of a circumstance does not hold you through your own conscious belief that it has any power. You are in the world but not of the world. You are in the world of a singular perspective of the Infinite Idea. You are not of it means, that you can only really be feeling and experiencing your Infinite Self. This demonstrates the phrase: It is not what you believe that is your power. It really, only, and infinitely is, that you the believer are the power. It is absolutely all you can experience and feel in reality.

This is free to fly, because this is your very reality.

> For we know in part, and we prophesy in part; but when the perfect thing comes, then that which is in part will be caused to cease. 1Cor. 13:9-10

> For now we see through a mirror in dimness, but then face to face. Now I know in part, but then I will fully know even as I also was fully known. 1Cor.13:12

BOOKS OF REFERENCE

BUSTING LOOSE from The MONEY GAME *by* Robert Sheinfeld

This book as I said has been very supportive to culminate all that I had learned and received from my expanded self. Mr. Sheinfeld reveals the map of the human game and its rules that are simply made up as well as what is your true unlimited state of being. He uses some quantum physics and explains what a holograph is and what it is in your world. He also gives a comprehensive step by step layout of claiming you power, called in his book, "the process."

THE HOLOGRAPHIC UNIVERSES *by* Michael Talbot

This is a book of opening up areas of thought that are far reaching and allow you to conceive of things that you may never have before. His back ground and references are enormous and I believe that it is a wonder ride to read.

THE FIELD, *by* Lynne Mc Taggart

This book is for those that are supported and energized by the understanding of quantum physics and may be more technical for some.

THE DIVINE MATRIX *by* Gregg Braden

I offer this book from the stand point that it clearly describes many of the quantum physic experiments in a very simplistic presentation. If one wishes to get a grasp on how certain conclusions are made in quantum physics it is a very helpful tool.

ABOUT THE AUTHOR

For 30 years I have experienced a wide range of spiritual teachings, both institutional and non-traditional. I have come from traditional biblical training to small religious sects of belief, some eastern philosophy, to Metaphysical and Science of Mind. I have a wide range of and have been ordained by some of my new age teachers with the Universal Brotherhood.

I have sought out and applied what I know to be True and Real. I allowed myself to be the living human experiment for what is real.

I understand that Words of "truth" become simple idioms and that words and concepts like Enlightenment and Consciousness are cache phrases that get lost in their over use. Living your life fully is to be able to totally and completely love, accept, and experience ALL OF YOU AND WHO YOU ARE. This is the only life and freedom that is worth the allowing. Knowing that as rare as it is to say; nothing is impossible, some things are, in reality. Such as, it is absolutely impossible to feel, experience, and know anything of your world that is not you and your Consciouness. This is the vantage point that life must be lived from if one wishes to live to its fullest and in your joy. I am everything that I have been looking for and so are you.

www.ingramcontent.com/pod-product-compliance
Lightning Source LLC
Chambersburg PA
CBHW020008050426
42450CB00005B/372